# Death and Continuity

**A comparative study of three modern Arabic novels by female authors**

Hoda Thabet

*Death and continuity*
Copyright © 2015  Hoda Thabet
Reykjavík 2015


National and University Library of Iceland ISBN: 978-9979-72-772-9

Printed in Háskólaprent ehf. 2015

ALL RIGHTS RESERVED. This book contains material protected under International and Federal Copyright Laws and Treaties. Any unauthorized reprint or use of this material is prohibited. No part of this book may be reproduced or transmitted in any form or by any means, electronic or mechanical, including photocopying, recording, or by any information storage and retrieval system without express written permission from the author Hoda Thabet.
http://is.linkedin.com/in/hodathabet

# TABLE OF CONTENTS

TABLE OF CONTENTS ............................................................................................. iii
Abstract ....................................................................................................................... v
1   INTRODUCTION ............................................................................................... 7
   1.1   The sublime in three Arabic women's novels ............................... 9
   1.2   An inner reading .............................................................................. 11
2   WOMAN AT POINT ZERO ............................................................................ 13
   2.1   Point zero ........................................................................................ 14
   2.2   Al-Saʿdāwī's language and the sublime ...................................... 16
   2.3   An alternative feminist mythology ............................................... 19
      2.3.1   Feminist revision of symbols ........................................... 21
      2.3.2   Opposing power by eye and hand ................................... 22
      2.3.3   The sea and the sublime ................................................... 27
      2.3.4   (Re)Birth ............................................................................ 28
      2.3.5   Limitations in the discussion of symbolism ................... 31
   2.4   The sublime to paradise ................................................................. 32
3   THE STORY OF ZAHRA ............................................................................... 37
   3.1   Ambiguity and the imaginal realm ............................................... 38
   3.2   Women's writing as political intervention ................................... 39
      3.2.1   Exposing the "prevailing delusional system" ................ 43
      3.2.2   The body in Zahra ............................................................. 43
      3.2.3   Decentering domination .................................................. 45
   3.3   Being and being-towards-death .................................................... 45
      3.3.1   Zahra and being/non-being ............................................. 46
      3.3.2   Being beyond death ......................................................... 49
   3.4   The role of anguish in becoming .................................................. 51
      3.4.1   Unveiling the unveiling of beings ................................... 52
   3.5   Authentic selfhood ......................................................................... 53
   3.6   Not knowing in the sublime .......................................................... 57
   3.7   Abortion and the maternal sublime .............................................. 59
   3.8   Flesh made abject ........................................................................... 59
   3.9   Sex is the silent other .................................................................... 60
      3.9.1   Exposing truth to disfigurement ..................................... 63
      3.9.2   Hysteria and depression ................................................... 65
   3.10   Sacrifice ......................................................................................... 66
      3.10.1   Subverting the order of the living and the dead ............ 67

|  | 3.10.2 | Blood, sex and death | 69 |
|---|---|---|---|
| 3.11 |  | Destruction as the origin of becoming | 72 |
|  | 3.11.1 | Near-death and the sublime | 73 |
|  | 3.11.2 | Denying the death drive | 75 |
|  | 3.11.3 | Culmination of the Dionysian ideal | 78 |

# 4 NIGHT OF THE FIRST BILLION .................................................. 81

| 4.1 | Irony and ambivalence | 83 |
|---|---|---|
|  | 4.1.1 Irony and the feminist sublime | 84 |
|  | 4.1.2 Is irony incompatible with sublimity? | 84 |
|  | 4.1.3 Negating evils | 87 |
| 4.2 | Parody and satire in the feminist sublime | 88 |
|  | 4.2.1 Satire | 89 |
| 4.3 | The uncanny in the sublime – Raghid | 91 |
|  | 4.3.1 The ghoul | 93 |
|  | 4.3.2 Absurdity, monstrosity and the uncanny | 96 |
|  | 4.3.3 Uncertainty and the uncanny | 98 |
|  | 4.3.4 The uncanny and the magician | 99 |
| 4.4 | Kafa's transitions | 101 |
|  | 4.4.1 Escape from war | 101 |
|  | 4.4.2 In search of identity | 104 |
|  | 4.4.3 The human situation as a whole | 106 |
|  | 4.4.4 Social death | 107 |
|  | 4.4.5 Some ethical questions in sublimity | 108 |
|  | 4.4.6 The surreal and the sublime' | 110 |
|  | 4.4.7 Kafa's maternal sublime | 111 |
|  | 4.4.8 Kafa's other self | 112 |
|  | 4.4.9 Ethics and the fool | 114 |
| 4.5 | Symmetry and sublimity | 115 |
|  | 4.5.1 Dunya as two women | 116 |
| 4.6 | The reader and sublime text | 118 |

# 5 DEATH AND CONTINUITY IN CONCLUSION .......................... 119

| 5.1 | The sublime as a feminist framework | 119 |
|---|---|---|
| 5.2 | Death and continuity in the feminist sublime | 120 |
|  | 5.2.1 The positive in the three deaths | 121 |
|  | 5.2.2 Ethics in the feminist sublime | 122 |
|  | 5.2.3 Value of ambiguity in the feminist sublime | 123 |
| 5.3 | Questioning the feminist sublime | 124 |
| 5.4 | Unmasking the logic of oppression | 124 |

**Bibliography** .................................................................................................. **127**

# Abstract

This study proposes the feminist sublime as a basis for interpretation of three modern Arabic novels written by women. Even though the sublime appears in classical Western literature, psychoanalysis, Biblical exegesis, Buddhist, Arabo-Islamic literatures and others, feminist objectives have led to the reconfiguration of the concept.

The novels analyzed are *Woman at Point Zero* by Nawāl al-Saʿdāwī, *The Story of Zahra* by Ḥanān al-Shaykh and *Night of the First Billion* by Ghādah al-Sammān. Myth and symbol, as well as tragedy, parody, satire, passive resistance, being and becoming, sexuality, sacrifice, and death in the three novels are discussed in the framework of the feminist sublime.

# 1 INTRODUCTION

This study seeks to view three modern Arabic works of fiction written by women through the lens of the feminist sublime. What does feminist mean? As it relates to literature in this study, it refers to a dual project for the personal and social betterment of humans. As a subject it is not so limited and this is a gross simplification. But for feminists, the personal may have extended meanings. The authors of *Does It Work? Feminist Analysis and Practice at Inter Pares* state that, "One of the central tenets of feminism is the idea that 'the personal is political'" (4). Reading can be a core feminist practice and I am assuming that a feminist reader may be reading not simply for comprehension. It might more often be part of an active process of constructing meaning and creating greater personal awareness. Thus, if for feminists, the personal is also political, it may be useful to have—as another tool in the toolbox—a type of reading which is not Western-centric and which is essentially feminist.

The *Inter Pares* research report goes on to make a point that will be central to the feminist sublime reading employed in this study:

> ... at Inter Pares we talk about the 'right to be'. And part of that is the right to 'become'... Women and all people have a right to be free from all forms of oppression and dominance... But it's also this notion of a right to become, to become yourself, personally and as part of a community of people, of autonomy and collective growth. (5)

Three novels are analysed and interpreted in light of the sublime: Imra'a 'inda nuqṭat aṣ-ṣifr, 1975 (*Woman at Point Zero* translated in 1983) by Nawāl al-Saʻdāwī, Ḥikāyat Zahrah, 1970 (*The Story of Zahra* 1980) by Ḥanān al-Shaykh and Laylatū al-Milyar, 1986 (*Night of the First Billion* 2005) by Ghādah al-Sammān.

Two of the novels investigated here are deeply influenced by the Lebanese war. The other, *Woman at Point Zero*, is set in quite a different battlefield, one without bullets but which nonetheless uses the body as the site of arbitrary pain and violence. War is an especially abundant field of inquiry into the sometimes shattering, sometimes ecstatic experience of the sublime and its attendant reconfiguration of personal, social, and gendered constructs. miriam cooke explains the effects of the Lebanese war on women's expression:

> Writing allowed these women to perceive a routine that did not deny the war but rather pinpointed a new logic, the logic of the bullets. This logic undermined previously unquestioned modes of behaviour and allowed for the emergence of a new *Weltanschauung*, a new social order and civic structure. (10)

The new world view suggested by Ḥanān al-Shaykh and Ghādah al-Sammān in the works examined here is, in fact, discursive, indeterminate and quintessentially a product of the sublime. Lyotard, who is much interested in communication and its effects, desires a sublimity that strikes us with its radical defamiliarization and presents us with something we cannot assimilate within the usual conceptual frameworks of our discourse (77). That communication may be a painting or a novel; it may be scientific, or any other form of expression, but in any case, the communication leads to an experience and an understanding—or at least a question—which lies beyond any structure of discourse as we know it. Lyotard calls this "irruption into the order of language of the unspeakable" (74), the differend. The differend, or the space within conflicting discourses, is what gives the narratives of al-Saʿdāwī, al-Shaykh, and al-Sammān liberating power. The ambiguity and interstitial character of the as-yet-unformed is the field of potentiality from which the new can be produced. The discourses in the novels by al-Saʿdāwī, al-Shaykh, and al-Sammān treated here are ripe with that productive potential. This researcher believes that the differend that makes itself felt in Arabic feminist novels has interesting implications for critical feminist reflexivity and the development of women's subjectivity.

Perhaps because the sublime event may take place beyond language systems, al-Saʿdāwī, al-Shaykh, and al-Sammān must employ diverse, ambiguous, and highly metaphorical figures throughout their works in order to communicate the differend. Lyotard's conception of the sublime as a bridge between differences, able to cross the chasms of culture and gender, and the unrepresentable, is relevant to feminist readings. Barbara Freeman and Patricia Yeager have extended Lyotard's notions to embrace more fully the feminist and subaltern consciousness, and to include the grotesque and abject amongst the contradictory discourses in the productive realm of the sublime.

Further, the process of becoming may be related to the abnormal conduct of our heroes in the three novels under discussion as regards their bodies. All three novels are situated around the heroes' bodies, all three heroes transgress body-related norms, and in some respects, all three women are "crazy."

Like the sublime, madness and death are often considered to be negatives—they are often defined by what they are not (a rational, living person is the norm for discussion). What Guven calls the "indecidability" of madness typifies Zahra's mental state during much of *The Story of Zahra*, and such indeterminacy forms an important part of her resistance to patriarchal pressures. What some regard as madness may share certain qualities with the sublime: ambiguity; uncertainty; liminality; and in-betweenness. These experiences are in common amongst the heroes in the novels analyzed in this book.

Firdaus in *Woman at Point Zero* and Kafa in *Night of the First Billion* also suffer from a sort of madness, or transgression against psychological norms, in their quest for becoming. It is a madness which progresses into a state of death, which will be discussed in this study, not as finality but as a point of transition toward continuity. Their refusal to engage in the everyday dichotomies (subject/object, male/female, self/other, and so forth) and attempts to straddle non-duality places them outside the confines of the patriarchal constructs, and therefore, mad or "dead," even if it is social rather than physical death. Their notion of being, or more specifically, of self, as ontologically interdependent and non-dualistic, can be perceived as seditious to the prevailing thought systems that entrap them into otherness.

## 1.1 The sublime in three Arabic women's novels

The interplay between the real/unreal and being/non-being is at the core of the feminist sublime probed in the three works under discussion here, a factor that has the potential to expand or enhance consciousness, and motivate profound changes in the lives of the heroes. As their subjectivity develops, so does their ability to act as agents of radical change. Even if those changes mean bringing about their physical deaths (as in the case of Firdaus and Zahra) or social death (as with Kafa); this could be considered to constitute another continuation.

An intriguing feature we will be looking into closely is the inclusion of the body. A thorough understanding of the body, especially as it relates to being and becoming, is crucial to a well-developed feminist subjectivity. The relationship between the body, power, knowledge, and discipline has been well explicated by Foucault and revised and extended by thinkers such as Judith Butler, Sandra Bartky, and Jana Sawicki. While some feminists reject Foucault's hypotheses, his conception of the wide-ranging and simultaneous generation of power and knowledge has been useful to this research. The Arabic women's writing under discussion here poses questions and provokes thoughts about the role of the body in forming identity, power relationships, sexuality, and being.

The literary techniques, styles, and narratives in the three novels examined vary considerably. Al-Sa'dāwī's seemingly unadorned, unpolished, rushed style somewhat obscures the careful construction in her reworking of masculine myth to serve feminist aims in *Woman at Point Zero*—a title uniquely appropriate to the theme of sublimity. The stark anguish in al-Shaykh's *Story of Zahra* courts Dionysian excess, exposing the raw forces of sex and death drives configured under repressive patriarchy and its ultimate expression: war. The absurdism and magical realism in *The Night of the First Billion* intensify the biting satire on the causes and effects of the Lebanese war. The wide disparity in composition, theme and mode of expression cannot, however, hide the commonality amongst the voices of these three diverse authors. The ways in which the body figures, the collisions of sex and death, and the depictions of women's growing awareness of themselves and the life transitions they undergo in order to understand and develop their subjectivity, are all different, yet share a sensitivity to the essential beingness, as well as becomingness in the sublime, that suggests a high degree of literary and philosophical sophistication. Their critique of women's subjectivity—in the fullest sense as described by Luce Irigaray, and not as a lack or deficiency of the male—

demands reflection. Therefore, it is hoped that this book will provide the reader with additional tools for critical feminist reflexivity.

The uneasy relationship between knowledge, death, madness, and eroticism is thoroughly examined by al-Sa'dāwī, al-Shaykh, and al-Sammān. Georges Bataille and Anne Dufourmantelle are important thinkers on sex and philosophy, and their works are liberally referred to in this study. Babette E. Babich's work on philosophy and eros in Hölderlin, Nietzsche, and Heidegger sheds further light on Heidegger's conception of being and love of knowledge as it relates to *eros*. Babich underlines the philosophical, "definition of the human as (the non-exclusively) rational and (not specifically) political animal. 'The human being,' as Nietzsche defines humanity, and as Heidegger quotes him, 'is the *always yet undetermined animal*'" (14). Accepting, understanding, and utilizing the undetermined nature of being may be viewed as an integral part of radical passivity espoused by Barbara Freeman and Patricia Yeager, which undermines male/female constructions and allows for new definitions of "woman" that go beyond current dualistic boundaries. Babich, citing Heidegger, further elaborates this aspect of being, which is distinctly relevant to a sublime reading of Arabic women's writing: "such an undetermined being must find 'a passage beyond himself,' and 'for this reason the bridge must be found to that nature by which the human being heretofore can be the *surpassing* of his former and last nature.' That bridge is "sheer, active transcendence" (84). Thus, both passivity and active transcendence are implicated in the feminist sublime found in the works of the three authors discussed here. References to a feminist sublime are by no means intended to suggest that this particular configuration of the sublime belongs only to women. The term is used to distinguish it from the classical and neoclassical accounts of the sublime, and by its very nature is theoretically open to any and all.

The highly imaginative texts of al-Sa'dāwī, al-Shaykh, and al-Sammān emphasize the importance of the imaginal realm in the feminist sublime. "Imaginal" is a word much used by Henry Corbin in his works on Islamic philosophy. To enter the *mundus imaginalis* or imaginal realm requires a painful, subtle and difficult personal transformation and embraced powerlessness, the ability to not know. Corbin explains that "the current attitude is to oppose the real to the imaginary as though to the unreal" (13), denying the trans-sensory power of the active imagination which transmutes the sensory into the symbolic (80). The visionary and very real aspect of the creative imagination seems to have been somewhat overlooked in the works under discussion here. Few reviews of al-Sa'dāwī's work, for example, praise her imagination: the "factual," biographical aspects of her work, and the degree to which her fiction may properly be regarded as socio-cultural artifact, are much discussed and sometimes deprecated. But her imagination is seldom praised for its fruitfulness and ability to mediate between the real and unreal, the spiritual and the physical. This is the realm where binary oppositions can be subsumed by new conceptions of being, new definitions of self. Islamic philosophy regards the cultivation of "the theoretical dimension of the intellect" (Azadpur 6) as a necessity, and places great importance on the role of the imagination as a cognitive faculty. The conflation of imagination with fantasy in modern Western society is viewed with dismay by Henry Corbin. The imaginal realm may be conceived of as that field of thought which mediates between, the real and unreal, being and non-being.

## 1.2  An inner reading

The history of the sublime has roots in Asian, Islamic and Western philosophy. Its explanation of both the phenomenology and ontology of encounters with something perceived to be greater than the self—whether through violence, pain, fear, love or ecstasy—seems well adapted to readings of *Woman at Point Zero* by al-Saʿdāwī, *Night of the First Billion* by al-Sammān, and *The Story of Zahra* by al-Shaykh.

This study is more inward-looking. Feminism, of course, is both an inward and outward looking discipline, and indeed, the word "feminisms" might be better employed in order to acknowledge the multiplicities and differences that one tries to contain in a single word. In *Women's Liberation and the Sublime: Feminism, Postmodernism, Environment* Bonnie Mann points that

> It is the notion of reorientation that is provocative in our consideration of the possibility of kinds of sublime experience that feminists might want to affirm. As much as our intellectual and political apparatuses alienate us from connection with other persons and places under conditions of postmodernity, we are also confronted with powerful experiences that lay bare these same relations, which, after all make us what we are. (145)

Choosing an analytical structure that can accommodate both readers and writers from diverse backgrounds is a special challenge. The evolving body of feminist theory and criticism has much to offer, yet this researcher has been reluctant to use a framework involving preconceived Western ideas. An ideational structure that accommodates the transcendental homelessness which uniquely characterizes the novel may be found in the sublime. Arabic women writers, especially, have been at the forefront in exploring states of ambiguity and in-betweenness, and the often painful process of becoming.

Although certain passages are also presented in the original Arabic and the translators tasks are there reviewed, we will not be focusing in general on the changes in meaning that the three novels have undergone in their translations into English. They rarely impact upon the topic considered here.

The same spellings are used herein for the characters' names in the English translations of the three novels to facilitate readers' of the present works comparison to their sources.

## 2  WOMAN AT POINT ZERO

The opening pages of al-Saʿdāwī's novel center around two characters, a convicted murderer and a psychiatrist. The doctor hears of this extraordinary prisoner, who has refused a pardon that would have commuted her death sentence. The mystery and strength of the convict, Firdaus, arouses the doctor's mind and emotions, and she becomes desperate to see Firdaus. After numerous refusals, Firdaus consents to see the doctor in order to tell her story before she is silenced forever. She recounts her childhood in a poor village, her childhood friend Mohammadain, with whom she played bride and bridegroom, and subsequently, her harrowing female genital mutilation, after which she was not allowed to play with Mohammadain.

Her parents having passed away at an early age, she moves to Cairo to live with her uncle. His relationship with her is not quite avuncular, as they sleep in the same bed, and he does the same things to her that Mohammadain had done—only now, her body no longer feels the pleasure it once did. He is a scholar, and she is allowed to study. She works hard at school, believing that an education will make a difference in her life. Her life is disrupted by her uncle's marriage to a woman who does not like having Firdaus in the house. Her uncle and aunt plan to marry her, without her consent, to an aging and repulsive uncle of her aunt's. Firdaus runs away from a home which is no longer a home to her, but returns after an experience on the street that scares her. She marries the bitter, angry, old Sheikh Mahmoud, who watches every morsel she eats, out of extreme meanness. He frequently shouts at her and beats her brutally; her life is unbearable, so Firdaus takes the bold step of running away.

She can flee her husband, but cannot escape the discrimination, limitations, and abuse she experiences as a young woman trying to make an independent, worthwhile life on her own in Cairo. Nearly everyone she meets is predatory, openly or covertly. One of her first experiences as a runaway woman, without a male protector, is meeting a man at a coffee shop, Bayoumi, who is the owner of the shop. Seemingly kind, he actually holds her captive in his flat, beats her savagely, and brings his friends there to rape her. A neighbor helps her to escape by bringing a carpenter to break open the door.

With nowhere to go, Firdaus meets Sharifa Salah el Dine, an expensive prostitute who teaches Firdaus the trade. Beautiful clothes, delightful food, and a good lifestyle are available to Firdaus, who realizes that even Sharifa enjoys only limited autonomy because her pimp can and does abuse her. Nonetheless, Firdaus persists in the profession and becomes very successful and independent. A wife was essentially a prostitute who was the lowest paid of all. At least now Firdaus was enjoying material comforts.

However, upon discovering that she is not perceived as being a respectable woman, she quits a life of luxury to work as a secretary. At the office, she loves a man, Ibrahim, who merely uses her for sex. Here, she is also taken advantage of for her body, but without the financial benefits of prostitution. Crushed and humiliated, she returns to her successful profession. Only as a prostitute, it seems, can she control her own body—she makes a point of refusing some rich and powerful men to assert her autonomy. It seems that she cannot simultaneously achieve respectability and control, but at least she can have some measure of power over her body if she transgresses respectable norms. However, this power proves illusory.

An abrupt end is brought to her story by Firdaus killing Marzouk, a well-connected pimp who is forcibly trying to control her and seize her money. He repeatedly beats her and threatens that she can never leave. He puts a knife to her throat to prevent her escape, and she ends up stabbing him.

The story ends as it began—with the words of the doctor. Thus, the story told by Firdaus in her own voice is framed by the voice of the doctor, who is dumbfounded and deeply affected by the courage of Firdaus.

## 2.1 Point zero

In light of our framework of death and continuity, the very title of al-Sa'dāwī's book invites discussion. The duality of zero/infinity is embedded in *Woman at Point Zero*. Zero simultaneously suggests nothingness or absence of being, and a concept profoundly threatening and subversive to the hegemonic patriarchal social order, for within zero lies infinite potential. "If you look at zero, you see nothing; but look through it and you will see the world" (Robert Kaplan 9). The philosophical context of zero may illuminate and add to the discourse about the personality of Firdaus, the condemned woman at *Point Zero*, and certain aspects of her experience.

Although the Arabs did not discover zero, they readily adopted it and are generally credited with having introduced the revolutionary concept to modern Europe via Leonardo of Pisa, better known as Fibonacci, at the beginning of the C.E. 1200's. Charles Seife posits that Europe's eventual acceptance of zero, not only as a number but also as a concept, helped to unleash the advances in science, art, and human knowledge known as the Renaissance. Zero made possible much that was hitherto impossible. For centuries, zero—with its intricate relationship with infinity and irrationality—had been rejected as heretical in the West. Aristotle had repudiated the Void in his philosophy of a finite universe, in which he had "proved" the existence of God. "When Christianity swept through the West, it became closely tied to the Aristotelian view of the universe and the proof of God's existence" (Seife 16). The steadfast refusal to entertain the concept of zero impeded the development of science and art; vested interests were at stake. "Before they could accept zero, philosophers in the West would have to destroy their universe" (14). The finite worldview dominated Western thought until the 1500s CE, although it took another two centuries to fully break down Aristotle's restrictions. On the other hand, Eastern and Islamic philosophers readily accepted zero and the void long before the West. Seife explained the mindset that refused to consider even the possibility of zero because it could destroy the prevailing construct of an orderly, fixed world: "it was not ignorance that led the Greeks to reject zero .... It was philosophy" (14).

On the subcontinent, the concept of zero held no such terrors and threatened no *status quo*. Robert Kaplan writes of the early days of zero, when the concept was under discussion but before the symbol for it was in use (44). An astronomer of approximately the sixth century named Aryabhata used the word "kha," which became the common word for zero. He used words like "sky," "atmosphere," "empty," to describe it. Around 830 CE in Mysore, a book was written dealing extensively with zero, again without a symbol, using "synonyms for zero, drawn from kinds and qualities of sky and space: depth, firmament, the endless, ..." (44). Already, nothingness is associated with the infinite. Some of the peculiar properties of zero were mentioned in poetic and philosophical language, such as the fact that zero divided with anything else is zero, suggesting that zero was "still part of discursive language rather than mathematics" at the time (45).

As we will discuss in this and the following two chapters, not only in *Woman at Point Zero*, but also in *The Story of Zahra* and *Night of the First Billion*, the lone woman is feared, shunned, disgraced—she is excluded from recognized society. She must live with her family or be married; she cannot decently live on her own. As Charles Seife highlights in talking about the strange properties of not being, nothing, or zero: "A lone zero always misbehaves. At the very least it does not behave the way other numbers do" (9). Joseph Campbell alludes to the pain and promise of the zero/infinity inherent in such exclusion: "From the standpoint of the way of duty, anyone in exile from the community is a nothing. From the other point of view, however, this exile is the first step of the quest" (224). Although zero figures prominently in *Woman at Point Zero,* it also bears a relationship to the other protagonists under discussion here in their encounters with the sublime. In al-Shaykh's *Story of Zahra*, for example, time and time again, Zahra stares into the void, but we will address her tale in more detail later.

Zero has many disturbing and even seditious aspects. Seemingly irrational and illogical, zero can spread like wildfire, asking more questions than it answers as it blazes through science, philosophy, literature and the socio-religious order. "The ratio of zero to anything—zero divided by a number—is always zero; the other number is completely consumed by the zero. And the ratio of anything to zero—a number divided by zero—can destroy logic" (Seife 13). Zero seems to have no substance, yet it has the power to challenge existing paradigms, and to open a space for transition and transformation. It implies the masculine conception of the female in her book: chaotic, dangerous, nothing. Al-Saʿdāwī's use of the phrase "Point Zero" is at once suggestive of the ultimate nadir and infinite potentialities. Al-Saʿdāwī's narrative exploits the relationship between death and the sublime, sacrifice and rebirth. It is the connection between zero and infinity that makes this paradox possible.

In his discussion on the relationship between zero and infinity, Seife unites the dichotomous pair as both "equal and opposite": "The troublesome nature of zero lies with the strange powers of the infinite, and it is possible to understand the infinite by studying zero" (39). He further points out that when zero is multiplied by anything, one gets zero. But when dealing with this hybrid between the philosophical abstract and the mathematical, division does not undo the operation of multiplication: "Dividing a number by zero yields infinity; dividing a number by infinity yields zero" (39). Existential contradiction is suggested by the title of *Woman at Point Zero*: a point of overwhelming powerlessness, yet one that opens the way to transition and transformation.

## 2.2 Al-Saʿdāwī's language and the sublime

We have seen that language itself can create the effect of profound sublimity; as Roland Barthes said, "I am interested in language because it wounds or seduces me" (38). While it may run counter to some criticisms of al-Saʿdāwī's work, this study suggests that her use of language in this novel is indeed sublime. First, a note about translation is unavoidable, then we will briefly look at the force of her language, which since classical times has been considered an important part of the sublime. Then we will examine al-Saʿdāwī's use of symbols in some detail, as it is contended here that this novel undermines patriarchal symbolism and mythology, in order to reappropriate them for feminist needs.

It has been noted that this study addresses works by al-Saʿdāwī, al-Shaykh and al-Sammān in English translation in order to render it more accessible to the non-specialist English feminist reader. The original Arabic wordplay, assonance, alliterations and idioms are, perforce, outside this discussion. In some respects, reading any literary work in translation must entail significant loss. Cultural references, some by the use of a single word or image, cannot always be conveyed. Money and politics may influence how a book is published, advertised, and even how it is translated.[1] Clearly, far more is gained than lost by the translation of literary works, provided the reader ingests translated books with some care and that the motivations of the translator and publisher are concerned with the importance of cultural authenticity and its transfer from one cultural context to another. It should merely be highlighted here for the English reader that she is reading a transformed version of the novel, and al-Saʿdāwī's original use of language in creating the

---

[1] Juliet O'Keefe and Amal Amīreh have written about the differences between the Arabic and English editions of al-Saʿdāwī's The Hidden Face of Eve, suggesting, for example that the female genital mutilation scene was sensationalized to some extent for Western audiences.

sublime cannot survive the translation; instead, we are dealing with something different, but entirely worthwhile.

In general, the use of language in *Woman at Point Zero* is spare and elliptical—Firdaus is speaking, not writing, and the Doctor's brief disclosures are made with breathless rapidity, "Let me speak. Do not interrupt me. I have no time to listen to you. They are coming to take me at six o'clock this evening." (9) Firdaus speaks in an abbreviated, forceful style made necessary by her imminent execution, which makes for a compelling pace but which leaves no time for rhetorical devices, such as those espoused by Longinus in his view of the sublime created by noble and elevated language. Some critics have made the mistake of confusing al-Saʿdāwī's simple, direct, lean use of words with lack of polish. This researcher would remind such critics of the dictum attributed to Leonardo da Vinci: simplicity is the ultimate sophistication. Without clever verbal ornament, *Woman at Point Zero* nonetheless suggests craft and complexity, which is rendered less obvious by what the chief narrator does not say. In this story, omission is one of al-Saʿdāwī's best devices. Similar to the way in which an abstract painting demands the viewer's participation, al-Saʿdāwī makes the reader work, and a lazy reader comes away with the kind of shallow impressions that one may read in some critics' empty homilies about the book. The narrator does not describe anything but the barest fact of her genital mutilation by stating that "They cut off a piece of flesh from between my thighs" (12). The reader is often left to supply her or his own fear, horror, shock, disgust, anger, or humiliation. Without the reader's collaboration, the scene is over in a few seconds. Exquisite language would be out of place: this is Firdaus confiding, and at times, asserting, her own story in her own way with only a few hours remaining before her judicial murder. Even before the first appearance of Firdaus, the strength of her personality is felt: her words wound and seduce without artifice. "If the President of the Republic in person had asked to see me, [the warder] could not have been swept by such an overpowering emotion" (6). One is left with the sensation of having listened to someone with a distinctive, powerful voice despite the seeming absence of rhetorical skill.

In fact, this study suggests that the reason why some critics state that it is a pity that al-Saʿdāwī is so popular in the West (because she is not representative and is not amongst the best of Egyptian writers) is that her skillful use of language is so subtle that it can be overlooked. Quite rightly, Mālṭī-Douglas complains that much criticism of contemporary Arabo-Islamic literature suffers from a superficial analytical framework (9). It is hoped that the feminist sublime may offer a deeper framework for al-Saʿdāwī's writing, and that this study is merely a starting point in such discussions.

For *Woman at Point Zero*, Burke's proposal of the sublime through language is perhaps more appropriate than that of Longinus. Al-Saʿdāwī's use of symbols, allegory and imagery are the most overtly sublime of her techniques. The use of elliptical style or omission is a covert or hidden technique, one that belongs to a postmodern feminist conception of the sublime that is woven through much of *Woman at Point Zero*.

A number of the experiences described—or rather, not described, but only briefly, vividly outlined—by Firdaus border on or enter the realm of the sublime. Whether or not the reader follows her there is largely dependent on the reader's disposition and sympathies. While literature must always be comprised of collaboration between reader and text, al-Sa'dāwī almost abandons her readers, requiring them to move forward on their own into the liminal spaces created by the questions, conflicts and shocks in Firdaus's life. Once al-Sa'dāwī, through the voice of Firdaus, has suggested the path, she leaves the reader alone. Firdaus is a woman on a mission, with no time to spare. Either the reader can and does imagine the experience of genital mutilation, or she cannot and does not. The narrator will not guide the reader through her experiences with descriptive detail or make engagement with the sublime any easier.

*Woman at Point Zero* is not devoid of a rhetorical skill that is traditionally linked to the sublime, but it is disguised. Allegory and symbol are embedded in al-Sa'dāwī's sometimes disturbing imagery. Allegory comes from the Greek word, *allegoria*, meaning "to speak otherwise." In Angus Fletcher's study of allegory, he states simply that "allegory says one thing and means another" (2). With respect to the Burkean sublime, allegory came to be associated with its opposite, the symbol. John Lechte proposes that allegory has regained its importance as a literary device with the "rise in the interest in the notion of representation and the 'inexpressible'" (16). Allegory is indirect, transitive, intelligible, and expresses the particular through the general; symbol is direct, intransitive, sensible, and is a particular which comprehends the general (16). Joseph Campbell reminds us that: "The symbol is an object pointing to a subject. We are summoned to a deeper spiritual awareness, far beyond the level of subject and object" (136). Together, the contrary linguistic forces of allegory and symbol employed by al-Sa'dāwī contribute to the creation of the sublime through language. Joanna Zylinska states that "the ethics of the feminine sublime springs precisely from corruption, alterity and foreignness perceived as an intrinsic part of the experience of the self." (n.pag.)

Nawāl al-Sa'dāwī attacks the corruption and the poisonous effects of organized religion through her portrayal of its followers, male as well as female. Ferdaus's uncle, who "was doing what Mohammadain had done" (13), represents the religion as an institution in society. He is studying theology in el-Azhar and later "found a post in the Ministry of Wakfs, and married the daughter of his teacher at El Azhar" (22). His wife, who has a voice "soft not with gentleness, but with the softness born of cruelty" (22), represents also organized religion as her father is el-Azhar sheikh. She forces Ferdaus to marry Sheikh Mahmoud who himself by being a Sheikh is a religious figure. One day when Sheikh Mahmoud hits Fredaus "all over with his shoe" (46), she takes refuge at her uncle's house but he refuses to shelter her. His wife tells her that "it was precisely men well versed in their religion who beat their wives. The precepts of religion permitted such punishment. A virtuous woman was not supposed to complain about her husband. Her duty was perfect obedience" (46-47).

Al-Saʿdāwī attacks the social institutions through portraying their unjust practices against women. Each of the men who sexually abuses Ferdaus represents a particular subsystem or sector of society. Taken together, they reveal a complex of societal forms perpetuating injustice and oppression. For example: Bayoumi, the owner of the coffee-house, exposes patriarchy in his social lower-class system; the policeman who rapes her represents the corrupted legal systems; Ibrahim the politician who abuses her, reflects the corrupted political institutions; the rich man, who pays her ten pounds, represents the corrupted economic institutions; while the prince represents corruptions in the governments. In *Woman at Turning Point*, al-Saʿdāwī exposes the corrupted social system throughout all its sectors: private and public; rich and poor; civil and governmental; religious and political. We will examine some of the symbols and associated mythologies she uses, which make a short book—less than 120 pages in English—so dense, rich, and timeless.

## 2.3   An alternative feminist mythology

Because al-Saʿdāwī relentlessly exposes what she terms the "contradictions and the patriarchal, class and race discriminations embedded in the three monotheistic books: the Old Testament, the New Testament and the Qurʾān" and makes statements such as, "Religion is a servant to the political system" (145), she is often perceived as radically secular within her Egyptian environment. However, there is little reason to suppose that she is unaware of, and does not knowingly and deliberately employ, the archetypical symbols so profoundly implanted in her culture, particularly as they have long since lost their religious connotations and become cultural icons. Al-Saʿdāwī's fictional writings may well be part of a deliberate feminist project of appropriating predominately masculine mythologies and symbol systems in order to disrupt and transform male definitions of what it means to be a woman. As long as women are simply lesser versions of men, they cannot have a fully developed, positive subjectivity: they are defined in the negative. Luce Irigaray articulates the need to loosen the grip of religions that serve to enforce patriarchal power and culture, specifically male-dominated religions that perpetuate the dualities of male/subject and female/body. Rather than fixing on a masculine, transcendental God, Irigaray advocates the ideal of a divinity that is feminine, sensible and transcendental. Although her approach differs from al-Saʿdāwī, Irigaray understands the need to reconstruct religion and male definitions of women. Like al-Saʿdāwī, she uses myth and mimesis to illuminate the distorted logic of male/master/subject and female/slave/object. In a sense, Irigaray seems to embrace the ontopoietic sublime, while rejecting the transcendental. In *This Sex Which Is Not One*, she insists that women must themselves (re)create feminine subjectivity beyond the boundaries and without reference to the male-dominated paradigm. The new definitions of what it means to be a woman can only be developed by the inner progress of women and mimetic engagement with stereotypes. There are both inward and outward dialectic processes to be experienced individually and collectively. Therefore, for Irigaray it would be useless to attempt to define "woman." That definition is something sought by Firdaus, Zahra and Kafa, characters in the three novels that are our focus. As we have seen, the sublime can and does often dispense with the transcendental; the feminist sublime tends towards horizontality rather than hierarchy, and tends to create new notions of subjectivity, self-awareness, and the female body. Freeing some of the potential for becomingness, myth can be part of, or even trigger, the sublime. Further, myth is an important psycho-social marker, and may be considered part of the collective mind. It is a religious and cultural language, and a way to comprehend chaos and liminality in transitional periods. Irigaray uses Greek myth to foreground her concern with the damage inflicted by patriarchy on the mother-daughter relationship. Al-Sa'dāwī goes further, by employing primordial mythological signifiers that resonate not only in Egyptian but also in most cultures of the world. Al-Sa'dāwī's symbolism in *Woman at Point Zero* suggests feminine divinity and the reappropriation of ancient masculine mythologies. While the mindset of ancient Egypt may seem a world away, how much has human psychology really changed in just a few thousand years? While our belief systems seem to have changed drastically, is our "mental apparatus" fundamentally different from that of our ancient forebears? Perhaps symbols and myths are more important to the modern mind than we may credit.

Why reappropriate masculinized myths for feminist ends? Joseph Campbell argues the urgency of a new understanding of the basic myths of humankind, and their relevance and power in the here and now because great poems, allegories, and metaphors spring from deep within the human psyche and are part of the structure of our minds (141). Mythology may be so essential to the human mind and spirit that it is part of our traditional culture irrespective of where we were born. Modernity or rigid religious doctrine can each deny us our human heritage of mythological understandings. Campbell argues that the psychological need for mythologies is so intense and inexorable that if we do not understand the mythology of our ancestors, we will invent our own—by joining gangs, worshipping celebrities, etc. It is not the intent of this study to analyze mythologies from a feminist viewpoint, but if Campbell's contentions about the psychological necessity for myth are correct, it appears that women, always marginalized, have a particular need for their own emancipatory mythology, or at the very least, a reexamination of the patriarchal mythologies that may be embedded in their thought.

## 2.3.1 Feminist revision of symbols

While it may seem a stretch to discuss pre-Islamic symbolism in *Woman at Point Zero*, al-Sa'dāwī plainly alludes to ancient Egyptian signifiers in other works, such as *The Circling Song* and *Death by the Nile*. She told Hans Obrist in an interview that she feels passionately about what she believes to be the starring role of Isis, relegated by histories written by men to a supporting role in the drama of Osiris (n.pag.). Elizabeth Goldsmith highlights the fact that signs such as the eye and sun are prevalent in cultures around the world and may be considered foundational to human consciousness (xi). The eye and the sun are intermingled in iconology of ancient Egypt, and are also related to the egg. The inclusion of these symbols is no accident. Joseph Campbell asserts that such mythology springs from the human psyche and affects us deeply, whether or not we are consciously aware of the significance of symbols and their myths. This study suggests that al-Sa'dāwī's use of profound symbols is connected with identity, revelation, and the sublime, which is affective, and not attained through logic and reason. This researcher suggests that al-Sa'dāwī's "revelation as a fiction" (to borrow Campbell's phrase) can be a far more effective way to expose patriarchal thinking and its effects on both men and women than a fact-filled documentary.

Thomas Merton writes that it is through symbols that one can enter affectively into contact with one's deepest self and with others: "The true symbol does not merely point to something else. It contains in itself a structure which awakens our consciousness to a new awareness of the inner meaning of life and of reality itself" (116). The sun, the eye, and by extension the egg, recurrently employed by al-Sa'dāwī in *Woman at Point Zero* as discussed below, offer what Campbell called, "the imagery of a revelation as a fiction through which an insight into the depths of being—one's own being and being generally—is conveyed analogically"(136). Al-Sa'dāwī's language, seemingly as simple and straightforward as the oral story it conveys, carries weight and power in its high-velocity charge to the final act—sacrifice and redemption.

It may be appropriate to remember that early Egyptian writing systems were highly symbolic. H.T. Velde notes that the writings were not mere pictograms, but were endowed with certain symbolic qualities or *sophia* by means of which they revealed to the initiated contemplator a profound insight into the very nature and essence of things and an intuitive understanding of their transcendental origin, an insight which was not the result of reasoning but ... inspiration and illumination (2). Their writing system is simultaneously pictorial, phonetic and symbolic: it seems entirely appropriate that Firdaus, who grew up in a village where the way of life was essentially unchanged for ages, should employ primordial symbols such as eyes, sun, water, and hand. It also seems appropriate that al-Sa'dāwī should revisit and revise these symbols in a feminist setting.

## 2.3.2 Opposing power by eye and hand

The eye and the hand have special significance. Al-Saʿdāwī uses these signifiers to convey a wealth of meaning in the context of resisting the abuse of power. In Firdaus's early life, the eyes of Firdaus's mother have an almost mystical power which is rendered more anomalous in the context of Firdaus's often pragmatically deadpan voice. "I can remember two eyes. … They were eyes that watched me. Even if I disappeared from their view, they could see me, and follow me wherever I went …" (15). Her mother's eyes are so powerful; they exert a palpable force on the toddling Firdaus and pick her up when she falls, while learning to walk. The maternal eye is important on many levels. For nearly all her life, Firdaus has been subjected to surveillance, the possessive and controlling male gaze, eyes that render her object, othered, and abject. Her mother's eyes—disembodied, perceived solely as eyes—are unique because they are both watching and supporting Firdaus. Later, when she does not perceive her mother as supportive, she believes the eyes have altered and the new woman, who looks just like her real mother, is a changeling, "No light seemed ever to touch the eyes of this woman, even when the day was radiant and the sun at its very brightest" (17). Those early eyes were the single most memorable and salient feature which defined her mother, and constitute her first memory of her mother. On the other hand, Firdaus also watched her mother's eyes (15). The gaze has such significance in Middle Eastern and North African cultures that many studies have been conducted regarding it—it is prevalent in both what has been termed "high culture" and "low culture." It appears in myth and religion and in everyday, mundane interactions. The gaze can harm or assist: it can be loving and encouraging; fraught with desire; or it can be envious, dealing out illness or even death. Women and children are most affected by the power of the gaze. Veiling protects women from the male gaze, while the *khamsah* (hand with an eye in the palm) protects both sexes from the evil eye. The eye and the gaze are, of course, inextricably linked. Is it possible to use the gaze to oppose power?

### *2.3.2.1 The gaze and objectification*

The gaze in *Woman at Point Zero* is not exclusively the male gaze upon Firdaus: her own unflinching gaze is described simply, but creates a complex interaction of gazes. One particularly oppressive gaze is that of her husband, who watches her like a one-man Panopticon at mealtimes to make sure she neither eats too much nor wastes a morsel, "He kept looking at my plate while I ate," (45) she relates to Sheikh Mahmoud. Her uncle has married her off, essentially forcing her to sell her body for the price of shelter and a few stingy meals—rendering marriage an unrewarding form of prostitution. Firdaus's relationship with food, in particular the most expensive food, meat, has been problematic ever since she was a young girl watching her mother feed her father meat while she and her siblings went hungry, "I sat in front of him watching as he ate, my eyes following his hand from the moment his fingers plunged into the bowel until it rose into the air, and carried the food into his mouth" (18). The pattern is repeated with her own marriage, but the gaze is reversed. Instead of longingly watching her mother's preferential treatment at meal times, Firdaus finds that her husband watches her every move regarding meat.

The politics of meat as regards women under patriarchy is treated by Carol J. Adams in her classic *The Sexual Politics of Meat: A Feminist-vegetarian Critical Theory*. She links denial, metaphorical or actual rape or dismemberment, fragmentation, economic inequity, the worship of male gods, patrilineality, similarities between the manner in which women and animals are treated, and more, with meat-eating societies (59, 85). The subject will arise in more detail in this study, because control over meat—the coveted masculine preserve—is a recurring theme and cultural metaphor. Both al-Shaykh and al-Sa'dāwī suggest social injustice on a wider scale through domestic scenes of favoritism towards the male members of the family. Meat is allocated to boys and men. Girls go hungry. As a child, Firdaus watches her father eat, and stretches her hand to his plate. He strikes her. "I was so hungry that I could not cry" (20). Few needs are more basic than that for food; the deprivation is deliberately demeaning. Somewhat uncomfortably, al-Sa'dāwī also reminds us of the role of women in the oppression of women. The mother is complicit in valuing her husband and sons above her daughters, re-inscribing patriarchal values. When Firdaus can control her own food, it is an important turning point in her life. She buys a luxury—chicken—with the first money she ever gets on her own; she "sat down and started to eat it slowly, very slowly, chewing every morsel" (70). However, the cost of such control is high and she is still trapped beneath the gaze of possession, the gaze of her clients. Food, control, her identity, and her objectification through gaze, are all linked at a fundamental physical and psychological level.

### *2.3.2.2 The eye, circle and sun*
In Egyptian myth, the eye and sun have a close relationship, and significant connections with creation, sexuality, and gender. Hathor, perhaps the most maternal of the deities in an approachably human way, has a sacred eye. But the eye, the sun and gender are tied even more deeply to what Jung called the "universal images that have existed since the remotest times" (5). Perhaps tellingly, R.T.R. Clark calls the eye the "key to the religion" (227). A circle with a point in the center, a round eye, is the astronomical character for the sun. It may represent omniscience, and the shape is reminiscent of the philosophical symbolism of zero. Elizabeth Goldsmith states that it may have signified the ovum: "This is the 'Orphic egg', a symbol of the universe whose yolk in the middle of a liquid surrounded an encompassing vault, represented the globe of the sun floating in ether and surrounded by the vault of heaven" (58). Associated with the Eye of Ra, The Eye of Amut and the Eye of Horus, it may also be referred to as the Eye of God, The Eye of Providence, or the Eye of the World in Christian and Buddhist teachings. "As an omnipotent and all-seeing power, the image

of the human eye has been regarded in many archaic cultures as an archetypal representation of deity as well as of the entire cosmos" (Hocart 388). It is in this light that the eyes of Firdaus's mother are first represented, "as though sunlight was pouring into them from some magical source". According to Madhu Khanna (21), the symbolic syntax of the same sign in the Hindu hermeneutic system is both microcosmic and macrocosmic. It encompasses both male and female: the central dot is the generative principle, surrounded by the cosmic womb. There can be little doubt that al-Saʿdāwī is fully alive to the implications of ancient Egyptian and other religious symbols. In an interview with Hans Ulrich Obrist, she discusses her plays and asserts that Isis was the philosopher and her husband was her follower, but the story was twisted under patriarchal readings. "So when I started to reread ancient Egyptian history I discovered Isis in a way that was totally different from how the Egyptian writer Tawfik Al-Hakim wrote about Isis" (n.pag.).

When Firdaus speaks of her mother's eyes, they are not in a face; there are neither eyelashes nor the distinct absence of eyelashes. They are intensely black circles within pure white circles. They are incorporeal and thus may be regarded as deeply and even purely symbolic. All over the world, and especially in Egypt, the eye is "imbued with cosmic, magical, and psychic forces that can be transmitted to human beings and other entities" (Garry and el-Shamy 139). One of the most ubiquitous symbols in Egyptian thought for millennia, eyes are by no means limited to the Middle East and North Africa—eyes also represented a Neolithic fertility goddess in Asia and Europe.

The very young Firdaus, learning to walk, "clung" to her mother's eyes. "All I can remember are two rings of intense white around two circles of intense black" (16). Utterly reliant upon her mother, Firdaus perceives those eyes as mysteriously radiant, magical, and superhuman. Later, her relationship with her mother deteriorates severely and devastatingly. Irigaray interprets the destruction of the mother-daughter relationship as a result of male control over women, and suggests that strengthening that bond could be an important way to undermine male domination. She uses the story of Persephone, the daughter of Zeus and Demeter, in which Demeter and her daughter are subjected to the arbitrary and capricious power of husbands/fathers, to illustrate a contemporary problem. Irigaray recommends that mothers encourage their daughters' becomingness through the intersubjective dialogue that young girls seek. Firdaus, of course, receives no such encouragement and consequently, is psychologically crippled by her mother.

The early feminine, motherly character of this circular symbol seems over time to have been subsumed by masculinity, but in the case of the Egyptians, it has made an interesting detour. The pre-dynastic fertility and sky goddess is later absorbed into Atum, a bi-sexual being. Jane Garry and Hasan el-Shamy state that the well-known Eye of Ra is a form of Atum (140). Thus, the Eye of Atum worn by pharaohs represents, amongst other things, the transcendence of the eternal male/female opposition in order to become complete and whole. Overcoming the stultification of being, and especially thwarted becomingness, is a hallmark of the heroes in al-Saʻdāwī's writing. A number of al-Saʻdāwī's protagonists take desperate measures in their striving for wholeness and autonomy, perhaps none more so than Firdaus.

### 2.3.2.3 *The eye and hand*

Ancient connotations for the eye (and sun) have already been mentioned. However, socio-cultural and religious practices and beliefs regarding the eye are prevalent in the Middle East and North Africa today. The use of eye symbolism may also be connected with al-Saʻdāwī's preoccupation with the body. The gaze is laden with different and probably far more cultural and religious meaning in Islamic countries than in Western states. The remarkably ancient and widespread culture surrounding the eye and the gaze has even resulted in the adoption of the khamsah as a national symbol in a Maghreb state, Algeria. Modern Arabic numerals use an egg-shaped sign to denote five, or *khamsah*.

This lore has special significance for women and children, who are considered most vulnerable to the effects of the gaze. Thus the eye and its gaze have bodily, sexual, social and political meanings in the Middle East that may not be readily apparent in cultures such as the American, where direct eye contact is often indicative of frankness and openness, and seldom considered offensive, dangerous or physically harmful, (unless it involves staring or potentially hostile situations) The earliest gaze of Firdaus's mother seems to have been the only concentrated gaze Firdaus had ever sustained that was not harmful.

Complicating Firdaus's journey from object to subject, from what she is to what she will become, is the fact that the gaze is not passive. Seeing is a possessive act. Rosemary Weatherston writes of the importance of the gaze in the production of the master's/colonizer's knowledge, the construction of othered inferiority, and ultimately, the conquest of "subject peoples" (23). With the exception of Firdaus's earliest memories of her mother, eyes seek to control every aspect of Firdaus's life and body, as though she is a colonial territory, a possession. She undergoes constant and penetrating surveillance from her mean, miserly husband; from men who undress her with their eyes; from her jealous aunt and abusive uncle: "seeing guarantees knowing, and knowing is understood in the spatial and visual terms of observation, penetration, surveillance and spectacle" (23). As an abject spectacle, she is consistently reminded of her inferiority through the gaze directed at her body. She must take strong measures in order to de-objectify herself and establish her own subjectivity and becoming.

The connections between the eye/gaze with veiling and physical isolation, ways in which the Muslim female is discursively constructed through gaze, the politics of the gaze, and mutuality of seeing, has formed the subject of many studies, and it is not our purpose to delve into those deep waters here, but only to point out that al-Sa'dāwī's references to eyes can be understood on numerous levels (and with respect to the eyes/gaze of Firdaus's repellent husband, all the oppression and objectification that the male gaze implies is surely intended by the author). The struggle to break free from the all-powerful male gaze and to attain self-awareness and power over her own body requires formidable effort of Firdaus. Her courage consists of occupying a succession of contested and opposing spaces in order to reach a state of being that she is consistently denied. In the end, she understands that being a secretary is no improvement over being a prostitute, and neither beingness allows her the space for subjectivity and becoming that she craves.

### 2.3.2.4 *The hand and touch*
Al-Sa'dāwī freely borrows, subverts, and re-imagines mythological symbols to serve feminist purposes. Through allusion and allegory, she is able to suggest a great deal in just a few words; she intellectually and intuitively illuminates the unknown, chaotic, ambiguous spaces that her heroes must negotiate in their ontopoietic journeys. As a physician, al-Sa'dāwī has a unique relationship with the body, which she thoroughly exploits in her fictional writing. Firdaus's fixation on certain bodily symbols is almost certainly multilayered and potentially transformative. Garry and e-Shamy write that, "[b]oth the hand and the eye play a critical role in people's everyday social interactions. They are vital parts of a person's body that physically and symbolically connect him or her with the outside world" (142). We communicate with others and with our world through eyes and hands. The sensible and super-sensible connections of eye and hand experienced by Firdaus are not so much quotidian as part of her encounter with the mysteries of the sublime. The omniscient, compassionate, comforting eyes of her mother/goddess disappear when Firdaus is too young to process the experience. Her early relationship with her mother is destroyed so completely that she believes her mother has been replaced by another woman. Firdaus, speaking in her surreal, clipped, spare style duly reflected in the translation, "My mother was no longer there."2 (17) She does not dwell or expand on this, but leaves the reader to envisage the horror and shock that any child would undergo in such circumstances.

Firdaus's connection with the hand is also double-edged. Al-Sa'dāwī appropriates the hand in a way that runs counter cultural associations. Other than the hands of Mohammedain, which give Firdaus pleasure early in the novel, men's hands

---

2 In the original Arabic, this is p. 20: أين ذهبت أمي لم أعرف
In the original text it is 'Where did my mother go I did not know"; al-Sa' dāwī uses her language skills in reflecting Ferdaus as a confused little girl who is searching everywhere for her mother without knowing where she is; and also without knowing that she will not be there anymore. This is the voice of little Ferdaus who when did not find her mother around; still she had a slight possibility to have her back hoping, as most children do, that the missing mother is busy in some of her errands and will be back soon. In the translated version, Ferdaus speaks as a grownup person stating her knowledge about the fact that her "mother was no longer there".

violate and ruin Firdaus such as her uncle's; "His hand would continue to press against my thigh with a grasping, almost brutal insistence."(17) Devoid of *barakah* (blessing), hands are masculine instruments of violence, abuse and force. El-Sayed el-Aswad writes, "In some contemporary cultures, particularly Arab societies, the hand and eye represent archetypal notions of grace (*barakah*) and envy (*hasad*), respectively" (139). Al-Saʻdāwī inverts the Arabic archetype to explore and upset the balance of power. Both the eye and hand are disturbing, possessive, cruel instruments of patriarchal power. Always oppositional to power, al-Saʻdāwī creates no pretense of beneficence or grace in the hands that assault Firdaus. The clear, confrontational gaze of Firdaus is, perhaps, one of her strongest attributes in her quest for liberation. "From that day onwards I ceased to bend my head or to look away. I walked through the streets with my head held high, and my eyes looking straight ahead. I looked people in the eyes, and if I saw someone count his money, I fixed it with an unwinking gaze" (73).

## 2.3.3 The sea and the sublime

Both the doctor and Firdaus metaphorically encounter the sea. Al-Saʻdāwī uses the overpowering nature of endless water as a key to the sublime. Numerous authors have reflected on the sublimity of the ocean, including Edmund Burke, Samuel Coleridge, Sigmund Freud, and Joseph Campbell. Reminiscent of the origins of life and amniotic fluid, the sea is both treacherous and comforting. Firdaus speaks of the sea, and of a time before she was born. The content of ocean water can closely correspond with human plasma; water is familiar and yet unknown. The sea is a dark, chaotic, boundless expanse. Both zero and infinity reside in the sea. It holds the promise of life, purification, and wellness, and it also contains the threat of death. The Doctor in *Woman at Point Zero* is emotionally overwhelmed, and in a dreamlike, almost surreal state, "It was the cold of the sea in a dream. I swam through its waters. I was naked and knew not how to swim" (7-8).

Firdaus, however, is continually, "like an object thrown into a limitless sea, without shores and without a bed, slashed by the waters when it starts to sink, and by the wind if it starts to float" (16). She is falling, buffeted and pulled in different directions. "Forever sinking and rising, sinking and rising, between the sea and the sky, with nothing to hold on to except the two eyes" (16). The chaotic and generational aspects of the sea may be conceived of as essentially feminine in nature. Dangerous, even life-threatening, it is an integral part of the horizontal sublime that seeks to redefine the feminine without reversing the roles of male domination. The unknown is frightening, yet women's path to occupying the subjective space fully, what Irigaray deemed using the "I," means taking risks. The sea both takes away and gives life, in a constantly unstable environment. Al-Saʻdāwī shares her personal view of the importance of chaos: "The theory of chaos has become a part of world science.

The minds of women and men have started to assimilate the idea of chaos as being the other side of order, like night is the other side to day, death a corollary to life, and madness an integral part of reason" (73). The sublime may help to provide a conceptual structure for the turmoil and ambiguity inherent in transition, and the reconciliation or transcendence of dualities. Al-Sa'dāwī continues: "Transitional periods of chaos are inevitable, but we should learn how to live and deal with them, how to allay the anxiety, fear and insecurity that they often engender among men and women" (73).

Jung analyzed at least 80,000 dreams, finding that all were in some way relevant, and that they followed patterns. In Jungian analysis, the sea can represent the unconscious, the maternal, or the feminine, which includes receptiveness and intuition, creativity, fertility, and birth. The sea can be violent and deadly; hence it is also a symbol of fear, horror and death. Drowning may represent overwhelming forces, or issues regarding the mother (von Franz 159; Jung 227). Symbolically, both the Doctor and Firdaus experience near-drowning. When they describe their oceanic encounters, the Doctor is in a dreamlike condition, and Firdaus in a state of altered consciousness provoked by the imminence of her death. Although the triple narrative frame of doctor, patient, doctor, is a standard framework for presenting case studies, here the "patient" exerts a strong fascination over the Doctor, who loses her professional objectivity immediately. She is swirled into the anarchy of Firdaus's life and functions under the spell of Firdaus's personality from the earliest time of hearing about the prisoner/patient. The homoerotic references to the first time the Doctor was in love tend to show how unsettling and sublime she finds her meeting with Firdaus. "It was a feeling I had known only once before, many years ago. I was on my way to meet the first man I loved for the first time" (6).

## 2.3.4 (Re)Birth.

The radical transformation of the sublime involves more than symbols; it requires fear, sacrifice and even death as precursors to rebirth. Firdaus undergoes a pattern of repeated renewals or rebirths in the course of her narrative. Each one has the promise of a new life unfolding in "ever new modalities of intergenerative, symbiotic, interactive, communicative linkage" (Tymieniecka 14). Strongly connected with the feminine sublime—involving the simultaneous exploration of self/other, and the (re)presentation of the unrepresentable—Firdaus articulates rebirth both directly and metaphorically. Birth is an ordeal for both mother and child, and one of the most distinctively female experiences of the body. Spiritual or psychological (re)birth can also be the result of having endured pain, uncertainty, chaos, the abject or ecstasy. Marked by blood and bliss, the ultimately female experience of physical birth is reflected in the emotional experiences Firdaus undergoes:

> I sometimes wonder whether a person can be born twice... When I opened my lids again I had the feeling of looking out through them for the first time, as though I had just come

into the world, or was being born a second time, since I knew that I had in fact been born some years before. (19)³

Defamiliarization, described as, "the feeling of looking out from them for the first time" and, "being born a second time" can be part of creativity and becomingness, and it can be the outcome of creativity. Victor Shklovsky used the term "defamiliarized" of writing that uses strange and unsettling language and images to perturb and disrupt, forcing the reader to see things in new ways. Gabriel uses defamiliarization to mean a part of the creative process itself, which allows one to explore, search, guess, experiment, and hopefully, to discover (8). Gabriel seems to agree with Goldsmith's suggestion that defamiliarization may be an aspect of the Dionysian impulse—it may seem absurd, demented, or magical, but it is part of rebirth and creation. Al-Sa'dāwī may use this technique to throw the reader off stride, and entreat their creative and emotional participation. Ultimately, in the context of life of Firdaus, it is part of her becoming.

> Back in my father's house I stared at the mud walls like a stranger who had never entered it before. I looked around almost in surprise, as though I had not been born here, but had dropped from the skies...to find myself in a place where I did not belong, in a home that was not mine, born from a father who was not my father, and from a mother who was not my mother. (27)

Firdaus's abrupt, lean style is a sharp contrast with the rich images and self-reflexivity she employs in her narration. She describes the radical defamiliarization, a hallmark of the sublime, as rebirths, or as having veils removed from her eyes. "The movement of my hands as I tore the money to pieces, tore off the veil, the last, remaining veil from before my eyes, to reveal the whole enigma which had puzzled me throughout, the true enigma of my life" (107). Yet however naïve her language appears to be, she refuses transparency. Through the act of telling her story with deliberate ellipses, she refuses to be subjected to gaze and ownership and control. She keeps to herself the intensely personal details of her sublime experiences. The sublime has been part of her life frequently, whether in abject rape (and sex with her husband is merely legalized rape) or in her realization of the power she can exercise over men, yet she describes only

---

[3] Unfortunately, at this point the translation lets the reader down. In the original Arabic, this is Pp. 21-22:
أيمكن أن يولد الانسان مرتين؟. حين وضعت يدي على "الزر" وعم الحجرة نور الكهرباء، أغمضت عيني من شدة الضوء وصرخت، ثم فتحت عيني وخيل إلى أنني أفتحهما لأول مرة، أو أنني أولد للمرة الأولى، أو الثانية، فقد كنت أعرف أنني ولدت من قبل
-"I shut my eyes…I opened my lids" فتحت عيني...أغمضت عيني
In the original text Ferdaus shuts her eyes and opens her eyes, she does not open the "lid" of her eyes; she opens wide her "eyes". Opening "my eyes" reflects the power of discovering the truth; it is here that for the first time she sees her reflection in the mirror and discovers how much she hates her cultural reflection. Here al-Sa' dāwī is using her skillful language ability to create a rhythm between two opposite actions: "I shut my eyes" and "I opened my eyes".
-"I sometimes wonder whether a person can be born twice" أيمكن أن يولد الانسان مرتين؟
In the original text Ferdaus is asking a question; a sudden and direct question that reflects her state of shock and confusion similar to that when suddenly "light flooded the" darkness.

certain aspects of it, hints at it, and plays with her listener's expectations. "I became a very successful prostitute. I was paid the highest price, and even men of great importance competed for my famours" (97). Her journey to be able to say "I" and "you", which Irigaray insists upon as essential to developing a new subjectivity for woman, leads her through uncharted waters, and—like other women seeking self-actualization—she must negotiate parts of it entirely alone.

To create is to give birth, and this is both terrifying and joyful. Al-Sa'dāwī remarks, "Creative women know how to live with chaos because they understand that every creation is an inspiration that surges up out of chaos" (73). Being reborn is, in a sense, Firdaus's own creation. In another very real sense, it is forced upon her and the processes are not under her control. She finds herself imprisoned by patriarchal walls, and her answer is to (re)create herself in a pattern that starts with her childhood and continues throughout her short life. Ultimately, the annihilations and renewals of self that she undergoes are what Tymieniecka calls "devices of the logos in its dynamic effusion" (33), while Firdaus negotiates the feminist sublime, incorporating her horrific experiences into new becomingness, and experiencing the 'chaos' of the (feminine) generative body.

Through lived experience and the transformations of the sublime, the trajectories of Firdaus's evolution as an increasingly self-aware individual finally lead her to a realization that the Doctor herself, with all of her education, has not been able to grasp. The Doctor, who may represent an upper-class woman confronting her own limitations in the face of an overwhelming social, political, and cultural patriarchy, seems to feel herself inferior to the force of Firdaus's asserted selfhood as though she is "being an insignificant insect, crawling on the earth amidst myriads of other similar insects." (6) Firdaus attains an understanding that allows her to make the choices that create turning points in her life; she begins to understand the nature of her being and the potential of her becomingness. Following the flexible but paradoxical pattern of the sublime, that understanding in Firdaus's case, results in self-obliteration.

Other al-Sa'dāwī characters experience rebirth and completely new understandings of themselves. In *Memoirs of a Woman Doctor*, for example, the young physician realizes that her body is not `awrah, not something abject, shameful, to be hidden: "I felt at that moment that I was born anew" (33). Mālṭī-Douglas likens a scene in which the doctor and her boyfriend successfully deal with a medical emergency in which the patient urgently requires blood, to the life-giving process. "They will cure the patient and allow him to be reborn. As a couple, they are participating in the activity of birth, albeit metaphorically" (21). However, the doctor is able to preside over births in ways that are not open to Firdaus.

Becoming a prostitute under the aegis of Sharifah (with the double-edged meaning: "Honorable One") is a rebirth for Firdaus. The transformative moment when

Firdaus gets her own money for sleeping with a wealthy man, and spends it exactly as she wishes, is another rebirth, a new self-identity is born. Mālṭī-Douglas speaks of the potential for rebirth in Firdaus's story-telling (32). After her escape from Bayoumi, Firdaus tells her painful story to a woman neighbor. After taking a bath, Firdaus feels that her body is "soft like the body of a child born an instant ago." Water, too, seems to play a role in purification. "I realized that I was born anew, with a soft clean body" (46). Firdaus is equally unable to become a member of the upper - or middle - class. Her becomingness is constrained by the accident of her birth. She serves the upper class as a prostitute, but cannot be an equal. Her rebirth of herself as a middle-class secretary is also part of what Tymieniecka describes as, "The meandering transformative, transmutative, sublimating, converting operations of the logos of life…" (15). The courageous and radical transition to secretary does not liberate Firdaus's becomingness. She has merely exchanged one form of slavery for another. At last, Firdaus decides on the final rebirth—her own death. "After I had spent three years in the company, I realized that as a prostitute I had been looked upon with more respect, and been valued more highly than all the female employees, myself included." (81)

## 2.3.5 Limitations in the discussion of symbolism

Many scholars, including Jane Garry, Hasan M. el-Shamy, Stith Thomson, James Hillman, Maud Bodkin, and Carol Schreier Rupprecht, to name only a few, have contributed to the study of the relationships between myth, folk motif, psychology and literature. This brief discussion of symbols can in no respect do justice to the scholarship in this field, and is intended to provide the feminist reader with some associations and connections regarding images that appear in this novel. Al-Saʿdāwī's rich imagery includes the womb, crucifixion, and many others that have not been included here. Further, the details of ancient cosmogonal and mythic systems vary considerably across time and location, and fine points can be argued almost endlessly. However, what is of interest here is what Campbell calls the "great poems" underneath, a deeper understanding of the symbols and allegory in *Woman at Point Zero*, and indeed, *Night of the First Billion* and *The Story of Zahra*. The liminal, the uncertain, the unrepresentable and the unconfrontable, as experienced through the encounter with the sublime, may be the engine of feminism and post-colonialism in al-Saʿdāwī's fictional work. In this way, both writing and reading can be forms of dissent that rock the very foundations of totalitarianism.

The reflexivity that can be generated by reading al-Saʿdāwī's writings may be enhanced by bearing in mind her knowledge of mythology and her deliberate feminist reappropriation of it. For example, *The Circling Song* is even richer in allusion, symbol and metaphor than *Woman at Point Zero*. In the former novel, the separated, yet somehow inseparable, lives of the twin brother and sister, in which the author intertwines, tests, and plays with their identities, bodies, and sexualities, all juxtaposed against societal restrictions and patriarchal impositions, may be considered as complex as a Nabokov novel without the word puzzles. The circle in the title of the book, symbol of completion, perfection, zero, the unification of male/female, and creation, is of course suggested in *Woman at Point Zero*. The circle with a dot within it is also suggestive of the ancient bi-sexual gods in Egypt, and the unity and harmony of male/female. The wholeness achieved through the incestuous union of the brother and sister is haunting; both of their lives are so distorted and fragmented by patriarchal burdens that they have few options for understanding themselves and their potential becomingness. Marriage between siblings was, of course, common practice in ancient times, but in the case of *The Circling Song*, the sexual union of the brother and sister was a result of confusion, trauma, an attempt to overcome the imposition of otherness and the urgent desire for the completion of their fractured beingness. As with Firdaus, they have little means with which to explore or understand their subjectivity, identities and socially gendered constructions, however, their gender and identity issues are more complex than those of Firdaus because they are twins of the opposite sex. Al-Sa'dāwī thereby creates an ideal platform for exposing the re-enforcement of patriarchal oppression with each new generation of humans, and its destructive effects on both sexes from the time when they are very young. The sublime opens the space for what Campbell describes as, "cleansing the doors of perception to the wonder, at once terrible and fascinating, of ourselves and of the universe of which we are the ears and eyes and the mind" (140). Al-Sa'dāwī's appropriation and subversion of masculine mythologies is too important to be neglected. This researcher contends that an appreciation of the mythologies embedded, violated or reconfigured in al-Sa'dāwī's works can add to the significance of her writings.

Al-Sa'dāwī's words may have stridency, but they also carry urgency towards the birth of a society in which humans are not, as she puts it, "slaves"—a society in which both women and men are free.

## 2.4 The sublime to paradise

Al-Sa'dāwī uses the venerable model of the framed narrative for her modern story. In the final frame of the triple narrative frame (doctor-patient-doctor), the Doctor says:

> Her voice continued to echo in my ears, vibrating in my head, in the cell, in the prison, in the streets, in the whole world, shaking everything, spreading fear wherever it went, the fear of the truth which kills, the power of truth, as savage, and as simple, and as awesome as death, yet as simple and as gentle as a child that has not yet learnt to lie. (118)[4]

---

[4] In the original Arabic, this is Pp. 93-94:

صوتها كان لا يزال يتردد في أذني، يرج أذني ويرج رأسي، ويرج الزنزانة، ويرج السجن، ويرج الشوارع، ويرج العالم كله. يسبب الرعب في العالم كله، رعب الصدق القاتل، هول الحقيقة المتوحشة البسيطة بساطة الموت، بساطة طفل لا يعرف الكذب.

- "vibrating in my head" ويرج رأسي

It is notable that the expression 'vibrating in my head' is far from being powerful enough as a translation. In the original Arabic, the echo of Ferdaus voice is so strong and powerful that it "shakes"

The Doctor is so powerfully moved that she has murderous/suicidal thoughts as she understands some of the effects of the patriarchal hegemony that virtually strangles women at birth, "I rammed my foot down on the accelerator as though in a hurry to run over the world, to stamp it all out" (114). She also realizes that, in order for authority to maintain its relentless grip, it is not so much Firdaus who must die as the truth.

The temptation to view Firdaus as a martyr is invited by her refusal to ask for the commutation of her death sentence. Further, her very name underscores her martyrdom. Derived from the Avestan *pairidaeza* meaning garden, *firdaws* refers to the highest garden of paradise, where prophets, the pious and martyrs will live after bodily death. The fear of paradise and of the sublime seems to go together. Roberto Assagioli stated in an interview that "[m]any people seem to have voluntarily submitted to a spiritual lobotomy, to a repression of the sublime, a complete denial of the transpersonal self." His interviewer, Keen, inquired: "Why should people repress the sublime? What's so threatening about paradise?" Assagioli answered: "We fear the sublime because it is unknown and because, if we admit the reality of higher values, we are committed to act in a more noble way" (n. pag.). The spiritual growth and physical freedom that Firdaus seeks are unattainable in her society. She has undergone transition after transition in her quest, only to choose bodily death as the final transformation. Her martyrdom may be seen as simultaneously redemptive and dystopian.

In a richly evocative but spare style, al-Sa'dāwī's tale foregrounds ambiguity, the abject and the potential of becomingness. She contests the binaries of sexual difference while opening a space that goes beyond dualisms. Outside the references of antimonies, the sublime may offer new ways to see gendered positions, as well as Being-toward-death. Through "blurring the distinctions between 'subject' and

---

everything as an earthquake which causes destruction; it is not a vibration. Also, al-Sa' dāwī repeats the word يرج similarly to the ways that shaking happens in reality; it starts from a specific point and it moves to the next point and the next point like a series of falling dominoes. Here the voice shakes first the ear, then the head starts shaking, then the cell, then the prison, then the streets, and then the whole world. The voice is not "vibrating in", it is fully taking over; it is not shaking "in the whole world" rather it is "shaking" the "whole world". There is a vast difference between having a vibration in the cell and having the cell itself shaking and standing on the edge of being destroyed. In the first, the cell stays in its strong stillness; while in the second, the cell is neither still nor strong.
- "vibrating in my head, in the cell" يرج أذني ويرج رأسي، ويرج الزنزانة
In the original text the voice continues its echo in the ear which causes the ear to shake first, then the shaking ear leads the head to shake, etc... As we mentioned above, al-Sa' dāwī is using her skillful language to represent the impact of shaking as it happens in physical events; in the translated version "shaking my ear" has been omitted. Here the translator has omitted the repetition of the word يرج which is a very skillful method that al-Sa' dāwī used to portray the impact of shaking in the original text moving from one point to the other.
- "spreading fear wherever it went" يسبب الرعب في العالم كله
In the original text it is not "wherever it went" because this has such a vague meaning. What if it only went/reached limited places? What if it did not reach further than the cell and the prison? In the original text it is "the whole world" which is also another evidence of al-Sa' dāwī's skillful language. First the voice "shakes the whole world" and this is the cause for "spreading fear" in "the whole world" (that is shaking).
- "the power of truth" هول الحقيقة
In the original text it is the "horror/terror" "of the truth" that reflects the destructive and shocking power; "the power of truth" in the translated version connotes the sense of positive impact and positive power.

'object,' psychiatrist and case study, author and prisoner, biography and autobiography, fiction and documentary", al-Saʿdāwī also points to the difficult way forward for men and women who attempt to transcend the patriarchal bonds that imprison their very being (Lionnet 145). Nothing is certain, but to accept things the way they are is to continue in a living death. Confusion and bewilderment are better than the certainties offered by the patriarchal order. "Dissidence and chaos that disturb the status quo are sometimes linked to madness in the minds of many women and men, who fear anything that upsets the false stability with which they surround themselves" (al-Saʿdāwī 73).

One of the most famed works of the sublime in the English language is Milton's *Paradise Lost*. Al-Saʿdāwī makes the point that she writes in Arabic for an Arabic audience, and there is no evidence that her choice of the name Firdaus for her main character was a conscious or unconscious reference to Milton. The irony of the name Firdaus is painful and patent without making any allusions. However, it may add another level of irony to consider the Biblical and Qur'anic ramifications of losing Paradise to a systemic patriarchy that pervades every part of our lives—social, economic, political, and juridical, to name a few.

It seems worth noting that Victoria Kahn's essay on allegory and the sublime in *Paradise Lost* proposes rhetorical ambivalence and indeterminacy, an "unstable rhetorical structure that dramatizes the necessity of negation or difference to cognition" as inherent to Milton's project of sublimity (185). In an entirely different way, al-Saʿdāwī's narrative also embraces and encourages the exploration of instability, equivocation, transitions, and metamorphoses. While one critic stated that Firdaus was too close to a saint for comfort, others have seen her as immoral and deserving of punishment (O'Keefe 127). The author who can elicit such disparate responses merits congratulations. Milton has also been accused of turning morality upside down. Like Firdaus, one of the chief actors of *Paradise Lost* is charismatic and admirable in many respects. Firdaus is neither God nor Devil, but in *Woman at Point Zero,* Paradise is destroyed after a lifelong battle, an epic struggle on an intimate scale.

The great stories, lore, poems and songs that are associated with the symbols employed by al-Saʿdāwī in her portrayal of one woman's sublime may have the potential to reach deeply into consciousness, so that it can become everyone's sublime. Primal images, such as the sun, eyes, hands, and sea, and allegories such as rebirth, creation, and sacrifice, give the story of Firdaus a timeless universal quality. Rather than trying to reproduce reality, *Woman at Point Zero* both produces and elicits truths. It is not necessary to seek the real life counterpart of Firdaus, nor to see al-Saʿdāwī as the Doctor—reason suggests that parallels are plentiful. However, the social logic of oppression as it intersects with Firdaus's being and becomingness is in many ways more real than reality, more true than any collection of mere facts. Charles Seife argues that nothingness joins infinity and that our limited minds cannot fathom this. It is, perhaps, only through the sublime that this knowledge can move from an intellectual grasp to a realized, internalized and intensely personal understanding.

# 3   THE STORY OF ZAHRA

*The Story of Zahra* is divided into two books, *The Scars of Peace* and *The Torrents of War*. In the first book, which recounts traumatic incidents in her early childhood and later, we hear Zahra's own voice reveal incidents involving her mother Fatmé, using Zahra as a cover in order to commit adultery.

We have discussed some aspects of the Arabic traditions relating to the hand with respect to Firdaus. In al-Shaykh's novel, Zahra's mother is at first represented by her hand—she is not mentioned by name, but rather, in a shattered, fragmented manner, that is, by body parts as metonyms (Harbawi 9). There may be an irony in Fatmé's name: "…a splayed hand called 'Fatma's hand' is meant to ward off the evil eye and proffer protection on its bearer" (Harbawi 9). Instead of protection, her mother's hand keeps Zahra silent.  Her father, too, is reduced to an enormous head, looking for her but not seeing her. We have already remarked on the importance of the male gaze in *Woman at Point Zero*, which surveils, controls and negates women. We will not repeat that here, but draw attention to its importance in this tale. The female gaze—Zahra's—will be discussed later in this chapter. The young Zahra successfully hides from her father in a dark room behind a door, but he later beats her savagely and repeatedly over his suspicions that she is concealing her mother's infidelities. This early betrayal by her mother, and dread and fear of her father is reflected in numerous incidents through her life, until she changes radically in the second book, under the influence of war.

The fig tree, emblem of the Tree of Knowledge and the fall of man through Eve's indiscretion in Arabic lore, is introduced in the description of her mother's secret meetings and recurs in the narrative. Another symbol that recurs, the bat, may be seen as a symbol of the liminality which plays such an important role in Zahra's life (Harbawi 9).

In the first book, she finds refuge in the bathroom, where she worries at her pimples until they bleed as an uncontrollable obsession. Because her facial disfigurement will reduce her chances of marriage, her father chastises her and beats over this, consistently rejecting her. When she is old enough to work, she takes a job and lives a double life in which she has an affair with a married man, Malek, who promises to marry her. Under his influence, she has her hymen surgically restored twice, and undergoes two abortions. Malek means "owner" in Arabic, and he does indeed exert ownership over Zahra's body. Male ownership and power over women's bodies was also a point of critical importance in *Woman at Point Zero*, as Firdaus actively sought autonomy. Zahra's resistance takes entirely different forms, as we will explore in detail. At home, Zahra maintains the persona of "Zahra in whose mouth butter would not melt, who had never smiled at any man" (40).

She leaves Lebanon to live with her uncle, Hashem, in Africa. As with Firdaus, Zahra's uncle tries to possess her body. Zahra represents the homeland from which he is exiled, "a direct contact with that which he misses the most, and from the outset he clings to it with all his being" (Allen 245). Her only sanctuary is again the bathroom. While in Africa, she is persuaded to marry Majed, a man who is her social inferior and is dazzled by the simultaneous prospects of social improvement and owning a woman's body to have sex with whenever he wants. Zahra's story is told from her own point of view as well as Hashem's and Majed's. Majed is appalled to discover on their wedding night that she is not a virgin. The stress of the unsuccessful marriage is too great for Zahra to bear; she reaches a nearly catatonic state before getting treatment in a mental hospital.

She returns to her parents' home in Lebanon, now shredded by a civil war that invigorates her and gives her new purpose. In the second book, Zahra almost becomes a new person, trying to stop the death on her street by seeking the sniper who deals out death randomly. She becomes pregnant by him, and he advises her to get an abortion. At the close of the story, he has shot her. Just as her story is replete with ambiguity, the ending of her story is equivocal.

## 3.1 Ambiguity and the imaginal realm

In *Woman at Point Zero*, we witness a series of sublime encounters that lead to the death, or the union of zero and infinity, of the protagonist. In *The Story of Zahra*, the protagonist is revealed as an even more complex being, as we share the experiences leading to her psychological torture and disintegration, and finally, what appears to be her physical death, although there are questions about the finality of the story's end. This study attempts to situate her response to oppression in varying forms within the sublime, tracing the arc of her introverted, sensitive self as she struggles to achieve autonomous being and fulfillment. Embraced powerlessness, indeterminacy and non-dualistic being are explored. Al-Shaykh negotiates the imaginal world in a highly ambiguous manner. This researcher believes it is important for feminist literature to recover the lost imaginal dimension of thought. Henry Corbin, building on the work of Mullā Ṣadrā and other Islamic thinkers, articulates the patriarchal degradation of the imagination into mere fantasy. Zahra, al-Shaykh's hero, seems often to be caught between different realities, which may or may not be fantasy or delusion. The loss or diminu of the importance of the imaginal, that is, the sense of the imaginary that is also real, to both men and women may have significant consequences: "there has ceased to be an intermediate level between empirically verifiable reality and unreality pure and simple" (Corbin 181). The narrative voices in *The Story of Zahra* sometimes dwell in the imaginal reality. The imaginal level of reality is real, but not objective. It is in-between, transitional, and borders on the unreason, irrationality, unreliability—which have been rendered "female" traits in the reason/unreason duality. Thus, the recovery of the imaginal realm for feminist purposes may well constitute a fruitful field of inquiry.

The interrelationships between sex, sacrifice, and death are pervasive elements in Zahra's story, and they are intricately linked to what Bataille calls "the revelation of continuity" (vi)—that is, the underlying principle of religion, and the transcendence connected with sex and death. Firstly, we will examine her story briefly in light of critiques of the famous novel. Secondly, we will review *The Story of Zahra* from the perspective of philosophies related to Being, which this researcher believes are peculiarly well suited to interpreting this novel and, perhaps more importantly, to forming feminist enquiries. Thirdly, we will examine the themes of sex, blood, sacrifice and death in the framework of the sublime, Being-towards-Death and Being-beyond-Death. The extraordinary richness of *The Story of Zahra* and the importance to feminism of questions regarding the fundamental nature of being, which contains within it opposites and difference, invites detailed discussion of these topics.

## 3.2 Women's writing as political intervention

miriam cooke explains that the Civil War in Lebanon was unprecedented in the way it was fought; it "penetrated every corner of people's lives" (3) and nowhere at all was safe. The violence "tore into the calm of the boudoir and the kitchen" (3). The general exclusion of women from the public sphere became meaningless under such pervasive, unremitting ferocity. The wrenching together of the private and public was shattering. As we shall discuss, the deeply divisive character of war is embodied in Zahra herself.

Al-Shaykh captures the confusion between the outer and inner worlds, particularly in Zahra's own voice. As we will discuss, Zahra's mental and physical state reflect her environment.

In some respects, the structure of the tale is, like the hero, schizoid. Anne Marie Adams points out that the title suggests distance, "whether in English or Arabic, the title is purposefully ambiguous about point of view and content: Zahra's tale is both by her and about her. It thus belongs to Zahra, her uncle, her husband, and her brother" (206). The splintered first-person narrative shifts from person to person, and between times and places, in an unsettling yet revelatory way. Where Firdaus undergoes radical defamiliarization as a part of her encounter with the sublime, Zahra feels disorientation, withdrawal, and instability. At times, she sees things newly, but her vision reverts almost immediately and her attempts to start a new life are false starts—her old world crashes in on her. Zahra's view—the way she sees, what she sees—is a strong element in the novel, as we will discuss.

miriam cooke states that, "She allows no one, and particularly not men, to come close to her and floats alone over the surface of life" (189). What "others call madness" is an important aspect of the novel. There may be as many differences in reality as there are people to conceive of "reality". Which of those realities constitutes madness? Foucault's major work on the subject is of great interest to feminists, and his discussions of the changing social and intellectual constructs that define insanity are relevant to this novel. As we will discuss, al-Shaykh has imbued the narrative voices with ambiguity and uncertainty; the reader may think he or she understands what is going on, only to have the objective reality of the narrative voice become highly suspect. The conflicts between different conceptions of reality within and between the different narratives offer questions about the nature of one's personal reality and how it is constructed. Because of its link with the feminist sublime, the theoretical framework for seeing different realities in this chapter (and "seeing" is important here) is the realm of imaginal realities, rather than of madness or unreason. As we will discuss further, Zahra's own eyes and seeing are central to the novel.

Al-Shaykh subverts narrative conventions in order to explore different realities, and the ways in which we constitute our reality. Gerard Genette describes the difference between the diegetic and extradiegetic, that is the events that take place within and the events outside the narrative (10). Zahra as narrator and Zahra as character are often but not always the same. Adding to the confusion, we hear the voices of her uncle and her husband, suggesting deviant, divergent and questionable realities.

Numerous analyses have drawn the parallels between Zahra and Lebanon, demonstrating Ḥanān al-Shaykh's skillful manipulation of internal and external identification and symbology—in such a reading, Zahra is a person and a nation, a being and a sign "To Hashem, Zahra is Lebanon, and to Majed, Zahra is status, but she is not reducible to either alone" (Hughes 22). Terrible acts are done to her, and sometimes she plays a role in allowing them to happen. Hughes uses three modern novels, including *The Story of Zahra*, to engage with expressions of identity, as influenced or constructed by war, community, place, tradition and many other factors. She explores the metaphor of Zahra as Lebanon partly because it opens inquiries about how women's bodies are used, and how subjective experiences are shaped by sex and war:

> Although Ḥanān al-Shaykh's *The Story of Zahra* portrays Zahra as an allegory for Lebanon, to simply assert that Zahra is an object of paternalistic discourses on women and war is to seriously obfuscate the radical sexual and social spaces and practices carved out for acts of liberation practiced by Zahra at the close of the novel, practices, although liberating, ultimately led to her demise. (28)

Zahra-as-Lebanon is insecure, vulnerable, and betrayed both by others and herself. Anne Marie Adams posits that in this reading, al-Shaykh is actively undermining the masculine nationalistic discourse by remapping the relationship between nation and woman (202). Political and ideological allusions can be interpreted as being woven throughout the fragmented narrative, from Zahra's fascist, dictatorial father, to the red swastika of the Syrian Social Nationalist Party, and to her brother's commitment to violence. Men attempt to mold Zahra/Lebanon into the form of their various religious, political, sexual and familial agendas. They never actually perceive Zahra for who she is or grant her the Being she craves. There is much value in the political and symbolic reading of the story, especially as detailed by Ṣabāḥ Ghandour. This book will explore the fundamental nature of Being which may lay hidden beneath the political, social and sexual conflicts that are literally embodied in Zahra. In this study, it is understood that Zahra may be seen as an allegory; however the focus will be on elements of being/becoming, sex, sacrifice and death in the feminist sublime.

The violence and social disorder that surround her is a critical aspect of being and becoming for Zahra. Marianne Rita Marroum writes of entropy as it relates to the writings of al-Shaykh. Entropy and chaos in *The Story of Zahra* are psychological and physical, internal and external. The bloodshed, turmoil, and uncertainty outside Zahra's walls are reflected in her mental state. Marroum cites Mohamed Dīb: "war literature uncovers the collective unconscious of the people" (69). Al-Shaykh relentlessly reveals the unconscious, in a delicate multi-viewpoint narrative in which each of the voices gives their version of reality. Sometimes unnervingly, the diegetic and extradiegetic narratives separate and intertwine, as will be discussed later. Roger Allen questions Zahra's reliability in his *The Arabic Novel*, especially in light of the fact that she was given ECT, which can cause memory loss, and catastrophic deterioration of personality (234). The reader realizes the narrative ground is shifting, few things are really certain, in this story. Ghandour points out the postmodern essence of the novel because the supposedly neutral voice of the narrator is not neutral at all. It lacks "historical truth" and produces its own truths. Another interpretation of the complexity and multiplicity of the narrative voices is that they explore the little-discussed imaginal realm. Compatible with existing studies of *The Story of Zahra*, the conceptual framework of the imaginal realm will be used in this study to add a further dimension to the ambiguity employed by al-Shaykh.

Allen highlights the divided nature of the narrative: "While the first part of the novel is a narrative of silence and suppression, the second part portrays an environment of noise; all the demons have been released, and the resulting din is all-pervasive" (234). The narrative is divided in another sense. Ghandour calls attention to the difference between Zahra as a narrative voice and Zahra as a character, a distinction that is important to understanding "how the structure of the novel itself functions as a counter-history" (236). In fact, the two weave in and out and merge at times, giving a rare sense to the reader of intimacy with and distance from Zahra by turn. This literary device, along with the multiplicity of views, offers an important feminist alternative to simpler, more dualistic ways of thinking.

Zahra resorts to self-mutilation, which becomes obsessive. As an act of abjection, it will be discussed later in this chapter. It also reflects societal and gender conflicts, and John Knowles reads it as a form of resistance (15). While symbolic resistance is certainly suggested, the obsessive acts may also be a form of expression. On one hand, Accad notes that, "[w]ar creates such conditions of despair that writing becomes a necessity, an outlet and a catharsis. It helps heal the wounds" (6-7). On the other hand, language has failed Zahra. She kept a journal for a time, but whatever relief it may have brought her was not enough. Elaine Scarry posits that pain can destroy language, "the power of verbal objectification, a major source of our self-extension, a vehicle through which the pain could be lifted out into the world and eliminated" (54). Zahra is inarticulate in the face of incomprehensible pain, and the power of language is distorted by the endless lies by which she is surrounded—lies from her immediate family, lies about the war. Rūmā Kamāl Salām discusses Zahra's acts of self-mutilation as a desperate means of communication. The acts might reach through the terrible blocks of silence and perverted language. If, as Scarry and Salām suggest, pain destroys language, Zahra must find some way to express her pain. The constant picking at her skin is one symptom of how deeply disturbed Zahra is; additionally, for Zahra, abortion is "a form of self-mutilation and expression" (Salam 33). There is an additional dimension to Zahra's repeated abortions—she is perpetuating the pattern of her mother's life. We will return to her mother's abortions later, as a subversion of the maternal sublime. Salām further interprets the abortions as Zahra's effort to expel the abject in herself, as a form of total abjection. Her abortions have also been interpreted as hatred towards men—a credible assertion, but one which perhaps sheds little light on the depth of her psychological disturbance.

Zahra is an instrument of pleasure to her abusive lover; she is a class symbol to her husband; she is a link to and the personification of Lebanon to her uncle; an object of discipline to her father; and even when well-intentioned, they never actually see her or allow her to be who she is. The people in Zahra's environment project their own meaning onto her, and ignore her true Being. The body is implicit in this understanding of the parallel between homeland, war, woman and sex. Both internal and external restrictions prevent Zahra from acting as she wishes; both internal and external sectarian, social and geopolitical factors contribute to and prolong the war. War, which is supposed to free her, destroys her. Zahra is not the only symbolic figure in the novel: her uncle Hashem, the hero of the failed coup; her husband Majed, segregated by class barriers; her brother Ahmed, seduced by drugs and violence; her parents, patriarchal tyranny with only subterfuge and hiding as resistance; and her grandfather, the comfort and stability of tradition, yet oppressive to his own daughter, each embody both outward socio-political and inner personal symbols. This great reduction of the complexity of the characters-as-symbols is, of course, cursory and intended merely to give the flavor of this particular reading.[5] The Zahra-as-Lebanon, who has been violated and betrayed from outside and

---

[5] The symbolic reading of Zahra is in some respects reminiscent of the reading of *The Song of Songs*, which refers to Lebanon, in which its emotionally and sexually charged lyricism is understood as nationalistic and religious, reflecting transcendent experiences that are beyond our intellectual comprehension. In *The New International Commentary on the Old Testament: Song of Songs*, Tremper Longman suggests that the *Song* was composed by a woman, "as part of an extensive tradition of women who sang songs" (8) or that it is women's poetry, citing Brenner, LaCoque, Bekkenkamp and other scholars. In the *Song*, Christ takes Israel for His bride, an act which clearly gives sublime pleasure. Al-Shaykh inverts the metaphor in *The Story of Zahra*. The sacred Biblical union, which is political, spiritual, and physical, is mirrored by Zahra's experience of transcendent ecstasy at the hands of her sniper lover, the god of death and embodiment of war.

from within has resonance on many levels, including the political and post-colonial. In the framework of the sublime, however, Zahra as a symbol is not the whole story.

### 3.2.1 Exposing the "prevailing delusional system"

*The Story of Zahra* illuminates the ways in which the patriarchal machine devours men as well as women and children. The way the figures interplay with the heavily gendered discourse of nation-building and nation-wrecking, and barriers of class and education and money, highlights the "alliance, dominance, and subordination" within patriarchal hegemony—what Raewyn Connell calls the, "gender politics in masculinity" (37).

*The Story of Zahra* seems simultaneously to exploit and question women's writing as having the potential to radically transform. In *Cassandra*, Christa Wolf, retelling an ancient war distant in time but with modern feminist urgency, also refuses to accept patriarchal idealism (259). Zahra, too, reveals the hallucinatory, deceptive nature of masculine ideologies that construct the military meat-grinder, which demands the flesh and bones of Lebanese men and women of all ages.

Masculine domination relies on women as a source of power. Through much of her story, Zahra is overwhelmed by external forces, rendering her passive and submissive. Her body is sown and harvested by men who completely objectify her. As Christa Wolf puts it, women are a power resource to be exploited (294). Margaret Atwood expresses the importance of women in fueling the existing power structure: "Women, it seems, are not a footnote after all: they are the necessary center around which the wheel of power revolves; or, seen another way, they are the broad base of the triangle that sustains a few oligarchs at the top" (364). Zahra unwillingly and fearfully supports the male hierarchy; her efforts to protest lead her deeper into the mire, her efforts to change are thwarted. Wolf writes of, "the route of segregation" which is at the heart of Zahra's struggle (287). She seeks oblivion, she hides, she retreats into sleep or the bathroom, seeks to return to her mother's womb, to overcome the dichotomies that crush her. The space to explore her own subjectivity is never granted her, so she can only retreat into non-being, ambiguity, in-betweenness, in order to avoid confronting that which she knows she cannot overcome. Zahra has no weapons against the abuses of power that annihilate her. The woman who starts to say "I," who speaks in her own voice, and develops her own being, faces tremendous difficulties. Zahra exemplifies the complications and barriers to women's becomingness. Part of her becoming is gaining the ability to see.

### 3.2.2 The body in Zahra

Eyes have special importance for Firdaus, and in a different way entirely, they are essential to *The Story of Zahra*. The gaze shifts and falters, revealing and concealing. Zahra seems really to see for the first at the moment of her ambiguous "death." Allen describes the asynchronous nature of the narrative, "The 'triggers' which lead into flashbacks are particularly successfully handled, but perhaps most remarkable of all is the use of repeated verbs (such as 'seeing' and 'fearing') to reflect the obsessive nature of Zahra's consciousness at certain points" (243). But the eyes that see Zahra never really see her. For example, Ghandour points out the palpable fact that, "Majed has never attempted to know the essence of Zahra" (244). The same is true of the others around Zahra. The gaze turned on her, and her own eyes looking at others and herself, obscure, deceive and distort.

In the second part of the book, Zahra comes alive during the war. Not unreasonably, Valassopoulos interprets Zahra as a masochist. Masochism is part of the death drive, "a pain that is felt to be necessary in order to achieve any type of pleasure" (67). She stresses that for Zahra, the moment of sexual pleasure reconfigures her entire life, which seems incontrovertible (68).

Zahra says it has made her feel more alive when she is visiting the sniper (138). Accad's theories on the indissoluble link between sexuality and war serve to highlight the great importance of understanding sexuality, in spite of the reluctance of some to do so in a feminist context. While accepting Accad's analysis, the aim of this study differs. The objective here is to analyze sex and death in light of fundamental aspects of Being. Alan Watts suggests that opposition of male/female indicates "duality rather than sexuality"; the transcendence beyond dualities to a more fundamental level of reality is therefore, of primary importance to feminism (52). Sexuality as a key to Being-towards-Death and Being-beyond-Death is a vast subject and this chapter cannot hope to encompass it. However, it will provide an overview as it relates to *The Story of Zahra*.

For Ghandour, "The personal is political" and Zahra undercuts or parodies the patriarchal story of Lebanon (235). The narrative collapses the divide between the public and private spheres. Zahra as metaphor for nation invites feminist and political dialogue. "The violation of her body is invoked time and time again in the novel; and the memory of such violation is presented in a disjunctive narrative. Each time the invocation of her bodily violations takes place, her body is being violated again" (Ghandour 234). Further, Zahra's body is important to constructing the memories and histories of Hashem and Majed (241). As the narrative deconstructs the separation between public and private spheres, it shows that memory is both personal and communal, public and private. Memory is physically and psychologically embedded in the human body, the city, the body politic, and the collective unconscious.

Further, al-Shaykh's unremitting but delicate questioning of the nature of reason and truth undermines the very basis of the public sphere—politics, social justice and personal and national sovereignty. As Achille Mbembe points out, "[R]eason is the truth of the subject and politics is the exercise of reason in the public sphere. The exercise of reason is tantamount to the exercise of freedom, a key element for individual autonomy" (13). Mbembe considers that this articulation of reason/unreason belongs to "late-modern criticism," however, this researcher suggests that in principle, at least, it is based on Enlightenment ideals and that *The Story of Zahra* offers a philosophical way forward.

Although the story may be bleak and devoid of hope on one level, its multiplicity of viewpoints, simultaneous holding of opposites and difference, and interrogation of reason and truth move it away from the concept of an immutable (masculine) reason. The male/female dimension of the reason/irrationality dichotomy has already been remarked upon. Al-Shaykh opens the door to new feminist thinking about unreason and autonomy.

### 3.2.3 Decentering domination

In order to suggest the mutual and contextual coherence of a literary school, miriam cooke has dubbed Ḥanān al-Shaykh, Ghādah al-Sammān, Emily Nasrallah, Daisy al-Amīr, and Etel Adnan, amongst others, the "Beirut Decentrists." They were doubly decentered, or excluded: "physically, they were scattered all over a self-destructing city" (cooke 3) and intellectually, they wrote from a marginalized perspective, while men wrote from a central position (3). Although they were not conscious of belonging to any school or being related to once another—"they wrote alone and for themselves" (3)—cooke discerns a unity in their diversity, despite their scattered and fragmented voices (4).

The betrayal by patriarchy becomes more evident as the war progresses and descends into hyper-violent gang warfare. The later Beirut Decentrist writing reflects some of the effects of the degeneration of the social order that Zahra's experiences. The war liberates her. For example, the terrible fear of her harsh disciplinary father is reduced, and she is able to make some personal choices. Both Mona Fayāḍ and al-Saʿdāwī have underscored the importance of women reclaiming their role in history by writing. "Arab women writers have developed a number of strategies to produce a counter-discourse..." (Fayad 147). *The Story of Zahra* is a counter-narrative that challenges and subverts on many levels. Meredith Turshen suggests that the destruction of war invites creation (20). Women courageously stepped into the vacuum left by a broken body politic.

cooke sees women's war writing in the light of an intercession which contains the seeds of the possibility of transforming the social logic of patriarchal domination.

### 3.3 Being and being-towards-death

Al-Shaykh uncovers ideas deeply relevant to feminism, war, identity, sex and the body, by investigating the fundamental reality of Being. The nature of Being is elemental to the sublime, particularly as it applies to Zahra. Her conduct—both passive and aggressive—may be interpreted in the frame of the death drive; however, this researcher suggests that her story offers an opportunity for deeper analysis into being and becoming, as well as non-being and ambiguity. For much of her life, Zahra suffers from severe constraints imposed on her from without and within. Inhibited and unable to communicate, she is acted upon unscrupulously, but she is not only a victim, she is a willing or unwilling accomplice in her own victimization. Her wavering between being and non-being gives her character unusual complexity. Many of Zahra's own acts are inscrutable to her. She does not understand herself, and despite long-term symptoms of mental disturbance, no one helps her to understand herself or to avert total psychological breakdown. Her condition deteriorates to the point where something must be done, but she is merely given sedatives and electroconvulsive shock therapy, rather than counseling to uncover and help her to come to terms with what she has hidden from herself. Since much of her life seems to be lived through her unconscious, this paper uses a reading of the sublime that straddles Being and (un)consciousness. Being-toward-Death will be discussed more fully in light of Heidegger and Islamic philosophy, in the context of *The Story of Zahra*. This researcher contends that such concepts are essential to the greater understanding that feminism seeks of women and power, because it may underlie all other conditions: in order to develop what Irigeray termed the feminine 'I', we must unveil more about the fundamental reality of being.

## 3.3.1 Zahra and being/non-being

In part, Henry Corbin's philosophy of being and the sublime informs this research, particularly his understanding of ambiguous states of being and embraced powerlessness which pervade *The Story of Zahra*. Starting as a student of Heidegger, Corbin found in phenomenology the door to a deeper understanding of Being. The principles articulated by Heidegger (and to a lesser extent, Husserl) led Corbin to Mullā Ṣadrā, Ibn al-'Arabi, and Al Suhrawardi, amongst other important figures in Islamic thought. Corbin admired Heidegger's "radical critique of Western thought by returning to a more primordial understanding of what it means to 'be,' …" (138). Being, to Heidegger, is that which underlies all of reality; it precedes all other considerations because all considerations presuppose it. Without a proper understanding of being, no proper knowledge is possible. In the most simple predicative sentence "I am" the "I" presupposes being and the existence of the subject, even before the assertion "am" is uttered. Heidegger compares being to the very air we "breathe" (141). Beingness is at the heart of Zahra's predicament, and at the center of the development of women's subjectivity. In this respect, the opposing philosophies of Heidegger and Corbin march together.

It seems probable that fundamental questions of being are valuable for feminists. The proper field of operation for the radical reform promised by feminism is, without exception, every field of human endeavor, therefore, the proper field of enquiry for the radical gaze of feminism is the human being, that is, Being itself. Luce Irigeray's refusal to define woman, because the process of definition is both an individual and collective, seems to reflect that same philosophical grasp of interrogating the essentials that undergird all other questions which drove the intellects of Heidegger and Corbin.

From her first memories, Zahra engages with non-being. Indeterminacy is her weapon of protest against the binaries and rigidity enforced by her parents. The struggles of being-towards-death are overwhelming to her. Her sense of both external reality and selfhood is fractured. She says of her mother, longing to be so close as to be one with her, "I wanted to disappear into the hem of her dress…", but at the same time, she is filled with hatred, pain and bitterness towards her mother (8). Such early emotional conflicts are scarifying and deeply formative; the pain and scars they cause inexorably persist like iron bands around her mind until she obtains some emotional release through the sexual sublime. Even at a young age, her mind is turned inwards, introverted, as she tries to identify her anguish, to understand the suffering she is undergoing, "I would question myself incessantly, yet the nameless feeling persisted. Even today I still ask myself what was the nature of this feeling. Was it jealousy? Was it pity for my father? Or was it the fear that took hold of me…" (9)[6]. However, since she is lacking a framework for conceptualizing her experiences and feelings, lacking any guidance, she cannot understand herself. One of the underlying tragedies in her story is that the people around her never actually see her. They see only their projections of her. She herself—whoever she really is, whatever her genuine and authentic being may be—is utterly neglected, negated, and unacknowledged. We are left to wonder if Zahra's compulsive self-mutilation and disfigurement are an attempt to deny the Being that is imposed on her.

A corollary to the denial of Zahra as a person, as a human being with a mind, emotions and dreams of her own, is that her mind and imaginal realm go uncultivated. However often her father and mother invoke the Qur'ān and God, they appear to have grasped religious rather than philosophical concepts; instead of cultivating their daughter's intellect and abilities, they inflict damage upon her. Her father's rigidity is signaled by his adoption of Western uniform and his timepiece—that most Western of accessories, symbolizing all that is not native and natural. Zahra's sense of time, in contrast, is non-linear, emotional, and intuitive. In describing her mother's trysts with her lover, Zahra is confusedly aware of the impact these incidents have on her feelings and perception. Her inability to understand herself and to relate to her own experiences distorts her vision and her ability to think. The way she sees is often ambiguous.

---

[6] At this point the translation lets the reader down, since in the original, this is p.12:
كنت أسأل نفسي، والشعور الذي لا أستطيع إعطاءه صفة يلازمني. وها أنذا أسأل نفسي الآن ماذا كان هذا الشعور؟ هل كان غيرة؟ هل كان شفقة على والدي؟ أم أنه الخوف الذي يضغط علي
-"incessantly" باستمرار
This word is extra in translation, it is not present in the original.
-"Persisted" استمر
In the original it is يلازمني which means "haunting me".
-"nameless feeling" والشعور الذي لا أستطيع إعطاءه صفة
The name is a subject (subject vs verb, object) and the literal translation for the original is: "The feeling that I can't 'describe.'"
-"fear that took hold of me" أنه الخوف الذي يضغط علي
In the original text the fear is strong and powerful it puts "pressure/press" on her; this has a hidden meaning of being on the edge of getting crushed.

> These encounters made my view of things blurred, as if seen through rain-splattered glass or steamed-up mirrors. My thoughts were unclear and seemed to relate to nothing in particular. They could arrive at no conclusions. (9)[7]

Her inchoate mind is already in deep water, and no one around her grants her enough beingness as a human to perceive what is happening. They see her only in the specific and limited roles they have prescribed for her, and nothing beyond. Still describing her mother and her mother's lover, she says, "It was a feeling which shattered both reality and imagination" (13). This splintering of her very being, which grows to schizoid proportions, continues to haunt her most of her life, until blood, sacrifice and sex release her from the wounds inflicted on her.

Early in her life, a pattern emerges, which is perpetuated in her adulthood. The struggle between being and non-being becomes all-consuming. She flees into the bathroom, the only place where she can lock the door and exert some degree of control over her body and herself, where she sometimes rolls up into a fetal ball for hours or days:

> …each morning, I merely locked the bathroom door and stayed a prisoner, even as I used to seek refuge in the bathroom back home in Beirut when I was afraid of my father's penetrating eyes—afraid he would discover what I had grown into, afraid he would kill me. (24)

The masculinity of this relentless penetration and possessive, controlling gaze, marks her father's role in her life as an unreasoning patriarchal tyrant. She articulates "seeing, yet not seeing" and "being and non-being" as something she observes in others, suggesting that she is aware of this struggle in herself; at times, she yields to the forces that overpower her and wants to "disappear in time and space," cut off from all human relations and her own memories (22, 97). Henry Corbin espouses the interrogation of reality "through the intensification of one's act of being and presence", rather than non-being (23). Desiring non-being may be equivalent to desiring death, but what are we to understand by Zahra's death? There are contradictions suggested by the end of the story, in which Zahra the narrator describes the "death" of Zahra the character. Zahra says "he has killed me," which is an impossible statement that opens many questions (not least, as Allen points out, the narrator's reliability.) If we accept that there is a death on some level (including but not limited to the death of her body)

---

[7] In the original Arabic, this is p. 12:
كان الخوف يجعلني أرى كل شئ كأنه من خلف زجاج انهمرت عليه زخات مطر، وعبر مرآة تغبشت أثناء دوش ساخن. أفكاري لا تعود تستند على شئ ولا تطلب شيئا. إنها مشلولة تماما.
-"They could arrive at no conclusions" إنها مشلولة تماما
In the original text Zahra describes her thoughts as being fully paralyzed. Being paralyzed has further, deeper meanings that reflect powerlessness, and perhaps a hidden cry for help.
-"These encounters" كان الخوف
In the original text, it is not just "encounters" it is "Fear". Zahra is haunted by fear and paralyzed by fear. "The fear" "made my view of things blurred".

then the ending of the story leads beyond existential and phenomenological questions and into what Corbin and Sufi philosophers called the unveiling of the hidden, Being-beyond-Death. As we shall examine, Bataille echoes this when he speaks of going beyond objective awareness.

Zahra's decision to stay in Beirut and refusal to return to the village during the war is pivotal: with her parents gone, she is now free to experience the physical and psychological space of her home and the city at war on her own. For the first time in her life, Zahra is not subjected to the cutting tongues, judgmental eyes and minute control of family. She is free to possess and explore domestic space as her own, and can come and go without explanation to anyone. cooke describes waiting, rather than fleeing the war, as potentially "transformative and active" (13). For Zahra, the wait takes on an active stance, because she uses this relatively autonomous time to seek a new level of being and becoming. For too long, she has been marginalized and made nothing of, and this is her opportunity to *be*. She uses this time on her own to seek a sniper. "Being is the *transcendens* pure and simple"; simply being allowed to *be*, without interference, may be therapeutic for Zahra (Heidegger 62). As her being develops, so does her being-towards-death.

## 3.3.2 Being beyond death

For the purposes of examining and understanding Zahra's existentialist torment, Edith Stein is an important critic of Heidegger. To Heidegger, death was final, whereas Stein was non-materialistic. To her, death was another beginning, even if unknown. Maria-Chiara Teloni writes eloquently of Heidegger's strengths and weaknesses through the eyes of Stein. Stein saw limits to Heidegger's notion of Being-towards-Death which she referred to as the root of his mistakes: his failure or refusal to consider the structure and complexity of the human body/mind/spirit (220). Although their approaches differed, both German and French existentialists dissected "being" at a materialistic level, contemplating the return to nothingness after death. Reality was confined solely to the material world. Stein considered that this fundamental concept had not been developed to its fullest meaning, because she regards the human as both "a psychical and physical being" and not simply a physical being. Therefore, Stein complicates Heidegger's relatively straightforward Being-towards-Death.

In *The Story of Zahra*, a complex reading seems more rewarding for feminist interpretations, not because it is more optimistic, but because the non-materialistic dimension adds another layer of meaning to Zahra's struggle. Zahra's narrative conceals the complexity of her situation precisely because she herself is inarticulate and unable to grasp the sources of her pain and to understand her own nature. For both Heidegger and Corbin, truth is never something which is immediately grasped. It cannot be ascertained by judgments or assertions. It is something hidden, which must be unveiled in the reality of being. Zahra's transitions and transformations are not straightforward.

Zahra does her best to wipe out certain deeply painful memories, but their power over her is compelling. "I erase from my mind my return home after the abortion when I kept my feet and thighs pressed tightly together so that my father would not discover my secret" (30). For years, she has suffered a morbid fear of her father. He may be a two-dimensional character, but to her, he *is* a terrifying brute. Her fear of him since she was very young holds her in a vise and seems to have risen to a pathological level. Her conviction that he will not hesitate to kill her if he discovers her wretched relationship with a married man, and its abject aftermath, may be based on her projection of her father rather than a more objective reality, but it is *her* reality. It may have been instilled by or originally projected through her mother. To Zahra, it is absolutely true.

> But my father's image, coming into my mind, frightened me to the extent where I felt sure he would kill me should he ever find out. He would not hesitate, I knew, even if it meant him spending the rest of his life in prison. He was capable of severing my head from my body. (31)[8]

This fear becomes a part of her being to such an extent that it may have caused her to become excessively passive: she is unable to refuse Malek's advances. Perversely, her fear may have led her to transgress taboos. Now that she has transgressed, her fear is reinforced by the consequences of discovery. "No day dawned, in any case, when I didn't open my eyes to see the sun or the rain and feel scared stiff that my father might sometime find out the truth" (40)[9]. At no time could she feel safe. Later, she unflinchingly

---

[8] Unfortunately, at this point the translation lets the reader down. In the original, this is p. 12:
لكن ما أن تدنو صورة والدي حتى اتكهرب، وأتأكد من أنه سيذبحني لو علم بأمري. إنه لن يتورع عن هذا ولو قضى بقية عمره في السجن. إنه إنسان قابل لأن يفصل رقبتي عن جسمي.
- "frightened me" حتى اتكهرب
In the original text it is not fear she says, "I become electrified", i.e. as if she got hit by electric shock. Electric shocks in the case of Zahra have various hidden meanings. First it can cause her death, it is painful and it hurts. Also it is a reflection of the state or the reason for her psychological problems for which she was treated by electric shocks.
- "he would kill me" سيذبحني
In the original text it is not just a normal act of killing; it is slaying or slaughtering which gives the image of the victim being an animal; you kill a person but you slaughter an animal. Also in the religious and cultural setting slaughtering an animal (for example the story of Ibrahim; or at the Sacrifice (أضحى) festival; it is an act of sacrifice to become closer to God or to receive His approval/blessing.
[9] In the original Arabic, this is.p. 42:
أي نهار فتحت عيني على شمسه أو مطره وغاب عن فكري القلق والخوف من أن يعرف والدي بالأمر؟
In the translated text the sentence ends with a full-stop while it is a question mark in the original text. By making it a question, the author emphasizes the state of fear that Zahra is feeling. The question 'was there any day that I was not scared?' implicitly carries with it a hidden answer: no, there was no such day. But having the answer hidden, and stating her fears through this question, makes the (No) as a statement answer stronger, deeper and more reflective of her inner fears. Zahra's story is a double-layered story, no direct answers are provided, no clear statements; and this sentence reflects this lack of clarity that the reader experiences while reading *The Story of Zahra*.
- "feel scared stiff" وغاب عن فكري القلق والخوف

examines the role of her ego in hiding the truth about herself, and wonders whether her fear of her father was actually physical. "It was all part of a conglomeration of fear, of fear, above all, that my image of myself might be overturned . . . the image of which I had run off hundreds of copies for distribution to all who had known me since childhood" (40). The fear that pervades her being almost certainly causes her to take irrational measures to avoid her father's wrath—such as moving to Africa, which is no answer at all to the demons inside her. Zahra's passivity may be a gendered as a social construct, as Kolbenschlag analyzes it, and "a metaphoric spiritual condition of women–cut off ... from self-actualization and capacity in a male-dominated milieu" (5).

An excess of passivity may be a novel form of excess; in any case, it is unusual and al-Shaykh explores the ramifications of what some consider a feminine trait carried to extremes. We will examine some of the key concepts of both Being-toward-Death and Being-beyond-Death as they relate to Zahra's story.

## 3.4 The role of anguish in becoming

As a young child, Zahra's mother's conduct opens her to childhood trauma. Both mental and physical anguish mark her days and nights. Heidegger proposes that anguish in the affective state, "is based primarily on the having been, and belongs to the past," whereas Stein theorizes that, "anguish connotes the emotional state on the base of which the human being recognizes his own condition of dependence" (Teloni 228). She is dependent on her mother of course, but she is also dependent on her father. She is placed in a dilemma where she has no choice but to betray her mother or be an accomplice in her mother's infidelity to Zahra's terrifying father. Until her transformation towards selfhood, Zahra is always dependent: she is at the mercy of her merciless father; she is dependent upon her husband; her uncle; her lover. She is

---

In the original text the worrying thoughts and the place of her fear is in her head, in her brain. Moreover, it is this head, this brain that is being treated by electric shocks; it is not her feelings. In the original text the word "vanished/disappeared" is used to describe how fears have (not) vanished from her head and her brain (even though she was receiving the electric shocks). Also in the original text, there is fear and there is also worrying (in the translated text the state of worrying has completely been neglected.
- "might sometime find out" أن يعرف والدي
In the original text, it is a definite verb (to know) which leads to a definite state of outcome (the slaughtering act of sacrifice); there is no "might" or "sometime". The state of fear and worrying is not taking place because the father might/or might not discover "the truth"; rather it is because of a definite strong fear that he will know. And there is no mention in the original text if "he will know" sometime or one day; he will just know, and it will happen on the spot, so fast, so tense like an electric shock.
-"the truth" بالأمر
In the original text nothing is mentioned about "the truth"; who is telling "the truth" in the various voices that narrate *The Story of Zahra*? The reader is never able to discover the truth. What is "the truth" behind Zahra's abortions or losing her virginity? Would the father discover the truth that his daughter Zahra has been raped and sexually abused? In the original text, it is not "the truth" that Zahra fears her father might know; it is the "matter" the "thing"; as though this "thing" would be so shocking for her father "to know" that it remains in a state that can't be named or described or have any solid identification. It transports the mind to think about it. In the original text, Zahra does not fear telling "the truth" or for her father to discover "the truth"; Zahra fears her father discovering what actually has nothing to do with "the truth"; it is "the thing".

dependent upon the claustrophobic homes provided her by her parents and husband. Home, like nation, is a gendered construct which leaves her no escape-valve—in the merging of home and street, public and private, there can be no respite. Even in Africa, far from the war, there is no escape. She is ultimately dependent upon the war to bring her back to life. Thus, Stein's extension and revision of Heidegger's concept of anguish is appropriate to the "dailiness" of the suffering that Zahra undergoes. Zahra's lack of independence, autonomy, or sovereignty is as applicable to her as an individual as it is in the construction whereby she becomes a symbol of a nation. Georges Bataille also offers an explanation of anguish peculiarly relevant to Zahra's relationship with sex, sacrifice, and death (39). Transgressing taboo is an inevitable, primal aspect of the experience. These intense emotions constitute the metamorphic elements in Zahra's encounter with the sublime. Bataille discusses the feeling of self-destruction or "tearing" oneself in going beyond the objective reality, making explicit the role of such profound affects in human development and becoming a fully realized female subject.

If Bataille is correct in stating, "Anguish is what makes humankind, it seems; not anguish alone, but anguish transcended and the act of transcending it", then Zahra's suffering is an essential part of her transformation (86).

## 3.4.1 Unveiling the unveiling of beings

As long as she is unable to understand or exert the concepts of "I" and "mine," she cannot truly inhabit herself. She is liminal, alienated from herself and others. Most fundamental however is her lack of integration with herself, which makes her a spectator in her own life. Heidegger explains: "'Dasein' exists.10 Furthermore, Dasein is an entity which in each case I myself am. Mineness belongs to any existent Dasein, and belongs to it as the condition which makes authenticity and inauthenticity possible" (112). Zahra's being is thwarted. Its negated, undeveloped, frustrated and injured condition demands recognition. "…from beginning to end, I had been a mere spectator" (al-Shaykh 113). Zahra's attempts at socialization cannot succeed. However, socialization would only have been a mask or cover for her lack of subjectivity and inability to articulate, even to herself, the "I" of her being. Heidegger would probably have regarded the Dasein that is drawn into a superficial social life as no more complete or "authentic" than one who stays locked in a bathroom for hours or days at a time, completely withdrawn from the world. Dasein "loses its identity in the impersonality of the 'They'" (Heidegger 126). Being free of the "They" is essential to authenticity; despite her efforts, Zahra cannot achieve this, unless

---

10 The *Merriam-Webster Dictionary* defines Dasein as "factual reality or existence within the spatiotemporal realm." *Encyclopedia Britannica* states that it is "the human subject, which Heidegger calls 'Dasein' (literally, 'being there') in order to stress subjectivity's worldly and existential features" and that Dasein is "a concrete and historically determinate situation that limits or conditions choice."

she does so in death. We will examine the concept of authentic self and the sublime more fully later in this chapter.

We find multiple layers of unveiling the hidden in Zahra, until she ultimately goes beyond objective awareness. The differing narrative voices conceal, obscure and finally reveal. "Unveiling the unveiling of beings" is the phrase used by Philippe Lacoue-Labarthes. *The Story of Zahra* employs alienation, derangement, shock and other means to unveil sublimity. In his essay *Sublime Truth*, Lacoue-Labarthes identifies the Heideggerian judgment of the sublime on the origin of the work of art. "A great work of art, according to Heidegger, *unveils the unveiling of beings*; it accomplishes this by defamiliarizing, alienating, deranging, shocking, transporting, and retreating" (Azadpur 194 emphasis added). Estrangement, aberration, withdrawal and moments of transition mark Zahra's life story. There are fragmentary, brief times of more fully becoming: "It seemed that life could, in fact, be simple and beautiful..." (115), however, her budding transitions and becoming are ruthlessly suppressed. Her anguish reaches the sublime, but in a manner which is seldom straightforward.

## 3.5 Authentic selfhood

Henry Corbin says that Heidegger "allowed him to open the locks of being" (12). Corbin's extensive studies of Islamic philosophy, particularly the works of Mullā Ṣadrā and Suhrawardi, enable him to expand Heidegger's *Weltanschauung*, which regards the material world as the sole reality, and to impart to Dasein a dimension that transcends physical death. In effect, Corbin utilizes Heidegger's analytic framework as a central point in his study of Islamic philosophy to reach hermeneutic levels that Heidegger had not contemplated. Corbin finds close parallels between Mullā Ṣadrā and Heidegger. They shared a "single and unique preoccupation: they both wanted to grasp the fundamental reality of being (*khod-e haghîghat-e vojoud*) and justify it in a philosophical frame" (13). They also understood truth as something that was not readily apparent, something which had to be probed and revealed. For example, *Verborgen* (hidden), has "equivalents in the vocabulary commonly used in Sufism and Islamic philosophy, notably ...the unveiling of the hidden under the phenomenon" (8). Corbin and his fellow researchers Mircea Eliade and Gersholm Scholem identified precisely analogous understandings amongst Christian, Jewish, and Islamic philosophers and modern phenomenologists. While no claim for the universality of this system of thought can be made, the similarities amongst the conceptions of the sublime articulated by disparate individuals and groups, spread across both time and space, are striking. This seeming independence from a single and particular culture, along with its liberational potential, is the root of the choice of the sublime as a framework in which to examine works by al-Saʻdāwī, al-Shaykh, and al-Sammān.

For Heidegger, "Dasein is an entity which, in its very Being, comports itself understandingly towards that Being" (125). Dasein constitutes Zahra's urge to become fully subjectivized until she reaches either liberation or a state of psychological breakdown. She suffers traumatic breakdown when she is in Africa, her marriage a humorless farce. The walls between past and present, always wafer-thin for Zahra, have disappeared. Her memories are jumbled; everything is happening all at once. Temporality is lost, and with it, the orderly march of events, or at least the illusion of the order of time. This unbearable state cannot last, and she approaches the catatonic. "Nothing disturbed me. I no longer heard my uncle's voice, nor even his footsteps behind me. I couldn't even see him. It seemed as if I continued to sleep, whether I walked or stood" (37). In hospital, she again receives drugs and electroconvulsive shock therapy, swelling her face and lips, making her memories subside. "As if in a trance, I knew nothing except for the light prick of a needle in my hand. It hurt. ... I tried to speak. I could not form a word" (37). Being and non-being have become confused. As with the time she discovered she was pregnant by Malek for the second time, reality and unreality merge. "I was in a state where everything existed yet didn't exist" (38). Being and non-being have converged in the penultimate ambiguity, an intermediate and in-between level of existence.

Zahra receives drastic treatments only when her condition has become so extreme that it penetrates the indifference or inability or unwillingness of those around her to perceive her mental state (39). She does not receive support at other times, even though her breakdowns seem to be merely acute versions the unbearable anguish of her everyday life. She returned to the pretense of a "normal life," which was neither healthy nor sustainable. "Yet those electric shocks would eventually return me to being myself and help me to get back to my job at the factory and live a normal life in all respects as if nothing had happened, as though it was some other woman, not I, who had been for a spell in hospital…as they jolted me against my will and my tongue stayed imprisoned in its housing of plastic"…(39)[11]. She is fractured from herself, unable to experience Being unless it is through death.

---

[11] In the original Arabic, this is p. 41:
فأنا قد اهتززت رغما عني ولساني محجوز في بيت من بلاستيك. بعد هذه الهزات التي كان تغادرني وتعيدني إلى حالة عادية أستطيع معها الذهاب إلى عملي في الريجي وممارسة أيامي بكل تفاصيلها وكأن شيئا لم يحدث وكأن من بقيت في المستشفى لمدة أسبوع هي غيري
-"they jolted me" فأنا قد اهتززت
In the original text, there is no mention of "they"; she is in such a shocking state of shaking and jolting that it is impossible for her to recognize or to see any "they" around her. In the original text it is "I was jolted". The emphasis is on "I" and nothing about "they". Prior to saying "I was jolted" she says: "but I did not hear my voice except after I felt the electric wires":
لكني لم أسمع صوتي إلا عندما شعرت بأسلاك كهربائية
So it is actually Zahra's voice and the first person "I" that is reflected in the original text. لكني لم أسمع
صوتي in *The Story of Zahra* this is translated as the following "My own voice only returned momentarily…" Here the emphasis is on the returned voice; and it is not on Zahra being able to hear her own voice which is the main reason for narrating her story; is to have a voice.
-"Yet those electric shocks" بعد هذه الهزات
In the original text, it is "after these jolts" so as to describe Zahra's continuous state of physical and mental shakiness: "jolting". It is not about the electric shocks, it is about what those electric shocks would do to her (her state of beingness or not beingness per se. This sentence is a continuation of her previous state where she says "I was jolted"; and now she describes her state after having been continuously "jolted" and "jolted" and "jolted".

Majed's voice is heard, describing his perspective of Zahra's breakdown as it affected him, and from what little he observed. He noticed the gross actions, but not the finer indications of what was going on in front of him. He describes her frantic hysteria alternated by abrupt and complete withdrawals. "She stared into a void, stopped eating and drinking" (87). Not much given to self-examination, he acts on his desires even when he does not understand them: "I drew close and began to make love to her .... An hour went by and she was still as rigid as wood. At times her eyes would be open, at others her face seemed expressionless. It did not trouble me." (88)

Oblivious to (or in complete denial of) her mental state, he rationalizes his own and her behavior until her withdrawal is so extreme that he cannot explain it away as supposed guilt over her non-virginity at the time of their marriage. Even her being taken to hospital barely penetrated the thickness of his certainty and judgment about her. "It never occurred to me to wonder about her treatment since I considered I knew perfectly well what was wrong with her" (90). She can barely function. Instead of having a wife to take care of his needs, someone to share his bed and cook his meals, the roles are reversed and he has to take care of her. There is little trace of compassion or understanding. He sees Zahra only in relation to himself, and not as herself. Her attempts to socialize are premature and backfire badly. They invite people over to celebrate their wedding and, "[h]er laughter went on for a quarter of an hour. We all tried to laugh with her, but the attempt was false. Her movements were nervous, the expression on her face blank" (91). What is hidden by her expressionless face? The layered unveiling and revelations are complex and ambiguous.

Perhaps courageously, she tries again to succeed with Majed. Upon arriving at the airport, however, she immediately realizes the trapped level of thinking that led her to flee Africa for Beirut and to repeat her mistake in returning to Africa. She cherishes an illusion that she can "return to my own home in Africa, where I could become anything I wished" but discovers that the promise of autonomy is delusory (107). It is not her home, it is Majed's, and he is a stranger whom she hates (107). Her emotions overwhelm her and her ability to think clearly, to be, is instantly and profoundly affected:

> ...how did I come to be returning at this moment, or thinking of remaining another second in Africa? It was raining, my heart was raining, my mind was raining, pouring out the thoughts that filled it, trying to reason, to arrive at some logical conclusion. But I had closed off every escape route and could only see myself caught in a net as sobs broke in my throat. (108)

Zahra's self-awareness or her ability to articulate is increased by the time her uncle speaks with her about her marriage and previous lover, to the point that she now understands the role fear has played in her life. But she is not much closer to understanding her pain or how to deal with it. She is confused and rudderless:

> I have lived in a cyclone of uncertainty and fear. ... Why did I remain only a witness and spectator? It is not, my uncle, because I am frightened of your scorn or anger or silence that I cannot tell you. I cannot tell you because I simply do not know. (114)

However, her inhibitions are so strong that she does not utter a word to her uncle; her reply remains an internal voice.

Heidegger's notion of "authentic" selfhood depends on acceptance of one's "ultimate finality expressed by the concept of Being-towards-death" (126), which does not seem to play an important part in Zahra's development until the second part of her story, *Torrents of War*. War brings heightened awareness of life's transience, alongside the factual immediacy of death—unpredictable, random and violent death. But death saturating the environment will evoke differing responses even in one person, let alone different people. Zahra at first is oblivious. Not much gets through her walled off emotions, so she sees war only as it relates to her and not as itself; the war is just something that lets her stay at home without having to face the present or the future. "All I need to do is keep my real self hidden" (105). She overeats and refuses to change from her housecoat for two months, until some of the violence in the world outside begins to seep into her consciousness. As she becomes aware of others' suffering, she feels guilt and visceral horror. "Suddenly I shudder as it seems clear to me that everything in our lives is on the verge of disintegration" (128). Obliviousness is no longer possible. Doing normal things like going to the café, cleaning the house, and even being alive is an offence to those who have perished: "I should let everything in the place die a slow death, and my father and mother would also do better if they stopped eating and living, for why should life continue inside the home when everything outside is collapsing? (130) It seems that Zahra is progressing toward what Heidegger conceived as the authentic self, Being-towards-death. War is bringing about transitions in her innermost self, as she is pulled out of her alienation and into the world. Her *Weltanschauung*, her view of the world and her place in it, is undergoing radical transformation.

Zahra's mental and physical pace accelerates with the imminence of death. Does she actively pursue death in a headlong urge towards the completion her being-towards-death, has she grasped a more transcendent conception of death, or is she unaware and utterly betrayed? The author plants contradictory clues about Zahra's frame of mind.

> Our street, once ruled by the spirit of life, now has death for its overlord. Somewhere in the lower half of the street there lives a sniper who perches on top of one of the vacated blocks. How is it that death has come to rule over half the street, directing that a child will fall, a man or a woman will fall, each with a bullet in the brain, each one alive and moving, even laughing or crying, at the very moment when they walked into the sniper's sights? (132)

Not forgetting the horror and shock of such deaths, she presents her body to the personification of these deaths, the "overlord," the sniper himself. Overtly or covertly, her drive towards death and sacrifice is conflated with her drive for eroticism, which will be discussed in detail later in this chapter. If he does not kill her, he may rape her. He may do both. Nevertheless, she gives him her body to do with as he pleases. Her bold act seems to be part of her will to transcend her current existence, at whatever cost. She has gone as far as she can; she remains trapped and in a state of limited subjectivity. Is there a possibility of something beyond the bodily death, the nothingness, inherent in the materialistic conception of the end of being? Henry Corbin said, "Existence for these [existentialists] leads to death, whereas in the philosophy of Mullā Ṣadrā and Persian Islamic philosophy, existence leads to transcendence; death always leads to higher levels of being" (12). This type of non-materialistic transcendence is not necessary to an interpretation of Zahra's acts during the war, which verge on the suicidal, but adds a dimension worth considering to her struggle towards being. Even while being-toward-death, she may be progressing towards a higher level of being, the transcendence beyond death, and perhaps a different authentic self than that contemplated by Heidegger.

## 3.6  Not knowing in the sublime

From Longinus to Burke, Kant, Heidegger, Corbin, and Yeager, descriptions of the sublime have held an element of transcendence. Even where the experience is horizontal, non-dominating, and non-dualistic, the notion of extending beyond known limits or conceptions may belong to the sublime. Thus, the sublime can accommodate and represent transgression, death, sex, the abject, and the othered or marginalized. The mere fact of abjection, transgression, etc, does not in itself signify sublimity, as we have witnessed in Zahra's earlier, extreme abjection, which leads to mental breakdown and hospitalization. Like the silence that hides Zahra's mind from others, her amorphous, indeterminate passivity has been the key tool by which her story unmasks the harsh, unyielding binaries underlying patriarchal society.

There does not seem to be a name for the space Zahra inhabits: it is neither being nor non-being, neither reality nor unreality. It is not mere madness, although she ventures in that direction more than once. This intermediate level; which may have been known as the Imagination to Islamic philosophers, such as Ibn al-`Arabi, is apt to be misunderstood by a modern audience that may speak of imagination and Disney characters in the same breath. Henry Corbin laments the loss of the "intermediate level between empirically verifiable reality and unreality" (181). The imaginal world is authentic and real, yet subjective. Through Zahra's liminality and transitions, al-Shaykh negotiates these uncharted waters. Thomas Cheetham, a Corbin scholar, says, "Entry into the imaginal requires a delicate, subtle and difficult personal transformation" (n. pag.). Deleuze's conception of reality, which includes the real and the "virtual," strangely echoes the imaginal realm so important to Islamic philosophers and modern phenomenologists. Eva Aldea's theoretical model of Deleuze's ontology will be referenced more thoroughly in the next chapter, but is relevant to all three heroes, Firdaus, Zahra and Kafa, and perhaps to the development of feminist subjectivity in general. Eva Aldea (21) underscores the two-fold nature of reality, and the incompleteness of a sense of "reality that only takes the actual side into account, which allows the virtual to be 'reduced to a simple possible.'" She cites Deleuze's stress that the virtual must be "defined as strictly a part of the real object" – therefore, it is a "plane of immanence." To Deleuze, appreciation and grasp of the virtual side of reality is a move towards self-actualization, towards "reaching the full potential of reality" (Aldea 20). This is where, "our greatest freedom lies – the freedom by which we develop and lead the [virtual] to its completion and transmutation, and finally become masters of actualizations and causes" (Aldea 20).

Zahra's wide, indeterminate sense of being allows her to reach the virtual as well as the actual, the real and unreal. This plane of immanence theoretically allows for vast metamorphic potential. However, overcome by traumatic experiences, Zahra sometimes gives undue weight to the unreal and seems trapped in the interstitial world of the imaginal. Zahra's vacillations between being/non-being, and object/subject reflect her refusal of the patriarchal knowledge dictated to her. She knows that she does not know. Living in the field of "not knowing" is uneasy, but truthful. It takes courage to embrace powerlessness.

The failure to acknowledge the reality of Zahra's thoughts and emotions may be at the core of her repression. Denial of the reality of self is tantamount to the denial of one's humanity, which is an integral part of any oppressive project. To be effective, tyranny must dictate reality, and that reality must be unambiguous. It is this unambiguous knowledge or reality that Zahra's implicitly rejects. Through *The Story of Zahra*, al-Shaykh interrogates the simplistic, black-and-white reality so beloved, exalted and enforced by patriarchal oppression, contrasting it with infinite shades of grey, plurality, complexity, and ever-shifting beingness. Corbin expressed a truth which is, like Zahra, indigestible to totalitarian regimes: "Human *be-ing* is a project, not a fixed state" (116). The counter-history explored in *The Story of Zahra* through the shifting, transitional states of the imaginal realm is not aimed at domination and conquest, but at self-examination and development. The philosophy of *The Story of Zahra* accepts the co-existence of opposites. It unveils the hidden in order to grasp the fundamental reality of being, which is paradoxically found to be ever-changing. Much may be conjectured about the end of Zahra's bodily life. This researcher's preferred interpretation relies on Corbin's understanding of the "essential person," which in its "posthumous becoming and in its immortality perhaps immeasurably transcends the 'personality' of so-and-so…" (116). Perhaps Zahra's immortality rests on her refusal to engage in the dialectics of her patriarchal environment, her ability to remain both open and hidden, and most of all, her ability to not know.

## 3.7 Abortion and the maternal sublime

Jennifer Wawrzinek explains that to Barbara Yaeger, "the maternal sublime is the origin of transformation" (18). Al-Shaykh's subversion of the maternal sublime is abortion. Abortion as subversion of the sublime is extended to its furthest point by the act of the sniper, who kills Zahra and their unborn baby. Abortion crosses two generations, from mother to daughter, in *The Story of Zahra*. Zahra knows of at least one set of twins her mother had aborted, in the seven years between her brother Ahmad's and her own birth, "a set of twins, girl and boy, who lived but briefly in a porcelain soup dish after my mother aborted them" (26). However, Zahra's questionable reliability as a narrator has been noted by numerous critics. Elise Salem suggests that Zahra is "not necessarily to be trusted" (120) in general and on this point in particular. Perhaps the objective reality is not the one that matters most in this novel.

Yeager describes the "maternal birthing body as the epitome of expenditure without appropriation," with the result that "the grotesque and sublime cease to be oppositional" (18). This "spreading of awareness," rather than vertical transcendence, is posited by Wawrzinek as the essence of the feminist sublime. Rather than seeking domination over the othered, the feminist experience of the sublime is inclusive and embracive. Its refusal to dominate or appropriate the othered means that it is inherently open to the reconciliation of opposites, or in the alternative, to providing space for the coexistence of opposites or differences. The subversion of an expected reality—in this case, related to the maternal body, motherliness, motherhood—makes other realities not only possible, but also more real. These simultaneously contradictory realities are what al-Shaykh seeks to elicit in *The Story of Zahra*. Alan Milchman and Alan Rosenberg describe this *Auseinandersetzung* or relationship between seeming opposites or differences as, "bind[ing] together in difference what belongs together in separation" (10). The co-existence of opposites in the horizontal, feminist sublime is a consistent theme in *The Story of Zahra*.

## 3.8 Flesh made abject

Meat—that elite form of nourishment—seems to be the most masculine of foods. The notion that masculine prestige and animal flesh mutually reinforce one another, to women's disadvantage, has been explored by Carol J. Adams. As with Firdaus, Zahra is made abject to masculine values through the denial of meat. To well-fed Americans and Western Europeans, the concept of deprivation of status through the denial of food may seem strange. Meat is simultaneously the desired and the unattainable. Older women participate in the subjugation of the younger women using meat: the mothers of both Firdaus and Zahra forward the patriarchal project of control to the minutest level by exalting the males in their families and objectifying and abjectifying their daughters; the daughters are not good enough to deserve meat. Each and every meal reinforces the inferiority and the marginalization of girls and women.

Meat-eating, connected by Carol J. Adams (241) to violence and dominance, is both a symbolic and real demonstration of the elevation of men and the abasement of women. The lack of nourishment enforced on girls and women is a daily reminder of Zahra's inferiority at a basic level.

Thus, food—intimately connected with survival, home, the private sphere—is invaded and controlled by patriarchal values. Denial of the desired food is reflected in Zahra's passivity and self-effacement, and her later obsession with overeating. In a real and figurative sense, Zahra is relegated to eating only what her father and brother reject. The force and violence of the dominant male is validated by claiming meat as a masculine preserve, along with territorial acquisition and aggression as seen in microcosm in Zahra's father, and in macrocosm, in the war.

The enforcement of the masculine flesh-eating paradigm which constitutes Zahra's domestic deprivation and abjection is a mirror to the widespread social and political conflict that engulfs her. "Every evening it was the same. My mother would never give me a single morsel of meat" (al-Shaykh 11). Later, when she is given a piece of chicken, she is so excruciatingly embarrassed, that she cannot enjoy it, "despite its tantalizing smell" and her hunger (12).

In Zahra's story, flesh is made abject in many different ways, the most important involving Zahra's own body. Ann Adams elaborates flesh and abjection outside the realm of food. She points out that domestic strife and disturbance is manifested on Zahra's visible flesh, that is, on her skin (201). The site of concentrated loathing, ridicule and humiliation, in a perpetual circle Zahra worsens what her father calls her "pock-marked face" (25). Zahra simultaneously perpetuates her abjection and registers her protest against it by disfiguring her body.

## 3.9  Sex is the silent other

At times excoriated as pornographic, *The Story of Zahra* deals head-on with some of the patriarchal and philosophical implications of sex. It is a Dionysian rather than an Apollonian tale, exposing truth to disfigurement, hurtling towards tragedy through excess and the grotesque. The ancient Dionysian trope is subverted. It now totes a gun and masturbates in front of its sister, its orgies are violent and abject—it achieves a sublime of a different order. Dionysus is not less dangerous for being disguised by repression, and obscured by rigid patriarchal ownership and control of the feminine.

Anne Dufourmantelle writes that "Sex is the silent other of philosophy" (11). Al-Shaykh shatters the philosophical silence about the relationship between sex, being, and being-towards-death. Avital Ronell's introduction to Anne Dufourmantelle's treatise on the relationship between sex and philosophy, asserts that, "Philosophy has never gone to bed. Commanding the most recondite corners of experience…"

philosophy rarely gives due consideration to sex (x). "This centuries-long avoidance strategy has implications for our destiny. Why would 'sex' belong to what I would call an 'oblitature,' the space of thinking's disavowal?" (Ronell xiii). Evelyne Accad posits the deep-seated and elemental nature of sexuality in understanding war and peace, the construction of gender, and our very psyches (12).

Sex cannot continue to be the silent other. Sex and beingness overtly and covertly permeate her story, from Zahra's earliest youth to her death. Zahra's childhood introduction to sex through her mother's secret liaisons is traumatic. It pulls apart mother and daughter, changing Zahra's being forever: they are no longer as close as orange and navel. Zahra's identification with her mother is abruptly and painfully splintered without a chance for the organically gradual development of Zahra's individual identity. Accad explains some of the damage inflicted through Zahra's mother and her "abandonment of her every time a man comes along" (45-46).

Allen highlights the evolution of Zahra's relationship with her mother in the course of the novel, and the mastery of al-Shaykh's prose, in which she skillfully embodies the voice of a child when describing incidents which took place during childhood. The narrative voices thus heighten the sense of atemporality and explore the imaginal reality. Further, they give a sense of how seeking to define and understand a reality actually constitutes that reality.

Although their relationship matures, the terrible effects on Zahra of maternal abandonment and deceit before she is old enough to understand it do not seem to quite leave her. Her own sense of motherhood is destroyed. This study is indebted to Allen for highlighting the incident in Zahra's childhood when she turns in a blank page for a writing assignment on motherhood. Zahra unconsciously mimics and reenacts her mother's deceptions, abortions, and the secret life of the utterly oppressed.

Her mother abandons Zahra to spend time alone with her lover. Zahra is left to herself and her tears, bewildered and afraid; and later, to fend for herself against her father, the "Lord of the Tramcar" who has no scruples about beating her as a small child, demanding to know where she has gone with her mother (14). Her mother abandons her to the unappeasable, insane wrath of her father, not even taking Zahra with her when she flees to the bathroom for safety. As a very young girl, a pattern is already forming: Zahra hears her mother say she wants to die, witnesses her mother escaping the violent rage of her father by locking herself into the bathroom and Zahra herself wants to jump out the window to escape (16). Sex, the unspoken, violence, terror, and abjection are all painfully crowded in her earliest memories. Lacking an emotional or intellectual framework to process the information, she internalizes it and subconsciously re-enacts the Dionysian dance with all its existential peril and violence, but without the *jouissance*. As a child, Zahra's being is already marked with the anguish and silence that shapes her entire existence. Her silence is not mere absence or nothingness, but filled with the clamor of the unrepresentable. Jennifer

Wawrzinek explains that in the sublime, silence, "becomes a space where one hears an undefinable *Urgeräusch*, a subsonic noise that lies within and beyond silence, an index to the existence of that which and those who cannot be represented" (13).

Zahra's relationship with her uncle in Africa has incestuous overtones that she finds bitter and frightening. Reducing her to utter abjection, although this is absent from Hashem's narrative. Her inability to speak coincides with her inability to bury her wounds (23). When he puts his arm around her and tries to hold her hand in the cinema, she is pushed over the edge: "I bled beads of sweat. . . I bled like a fountain, felt like crying, like running away, like screaming until the movie finished and the lights came up" (23). She is not an innocent virgin suffering from nervousness at the unknown; she understands very well where his behavior is leading. Or does she? His tale differs from hers as much as any two of the stories in Roshomon—truth is relative, shifting and doubtful. Only the fundamental reality may be immutable, when we "discover our complete being through the recovery of its lost spiritual dimension" (Corbin 22). A reality that is true for Zahra is that her uncle routinely intrudes himself into her bedroom, lies down on the bed alongside her, tries to wake her and get her full attention. He even invades her diary, leaving her neither psychological nor physical space of her own (28). She becomes wooden—a recurring defensive act, she can only hide or go numb to avoid the anguish and distress, shame and embarrassment that entrap her.

Her self-mutilation has been a source of considerable conjecture among readers (al Masri 116). Is the obsessive destruction of her face a way to repel men and avoid having to confront the misery associated with sex? She is uncomfortable in the company of others, her hand always "automatically rises to touch the acne" on her face (113). For all her lack of beauty, her awkwardness and self-consciousness, Majed asks her to marry him at their first dance (29). They do not know one another, there can be no question of affection or even bare friendship—she is a socially acceptable means for him to have a woman's body conveniently close to hand whenever wants sex, and she is a means for him to rise above his lower class origins. Majed is a way for her to escape her uncle's unwanted attentions and perhaps start a new life in which she will attain some degree of autonomy. But wedlock is the beginning of a new nightmare.

> Dear God! The things that I feel whenever Majed comes close to me cold winds, cold, crowding me close with thousands of snails crawling closer, crawling across the mud as the winds blow ever more strongly, carrying the snails' foul odor which soaks into every pore. (93)

The monstrous, and extremes of revulsion, "the agitation and commotion of the soul", and confusion, and excess, have the potential to transgress and erode the borders of identity and authority (Longinus 45). Zahra's experience of the sublime is overwhelming—she is lost at sea. Her tears are like an ocean. "No sooner do I open my eyes than I wish I could close them again. I feel as if salt water is flowing in the space that surrounds me" (93). Seeing (and not seeing) recur at important points in the story.

### 3.9.1 Exposing truth to disfigurement

Al-Shaykh expropriates the Dionysian principle which celebrates the chaos associated with the female aspect of being. Philosophy may be reticent about sex, but religion is not. As we have seen, early religions did not shy away from dealing with sex and gender, especially as related to creation mythology—offering a confrontation with and transcendence over sexist domination that major religions tend to avoid, suppressing the female aspect of divinity, mystery and creation. Manly Palmer Hall asserts that the mistranslation of a single word in the Bible has caused the loss of an entire way of thinking: "[W]hen the plural and androgynous Hebrew word *Elohim* was translated into the singular and sexless word God, the opening chapters of Genesis were rendered comparatively meaningless" (372). Hall claims that the correct translation of *Elohim* is "the male and female creative agencies," which if true gives a startlingly different reading. His analysis of the verses of Genesis continues:

> [T]he plural form of the pronouns 'us' and 'our' reveals unmistakably, however, the pantheistic nature of Divinity. Further, the androgynous constitution of the *Elohim* (God) is disclosed in the next verse, where he (referring to God) is said to have created man in his own image, male and female; or, more properly, as the division of the sexes had not yet taken place, male-female. This is a deathblow to the time-honored concept that God is a masculine potency .... (372)

Zahra's father, who held the Qur'ān aloft while beating her mother with his belt until her face was bloodied, was plainly unaware of the feminine aspect of God. Zahra's reaction—her instinctive performance of Shi'ite grief ritual—demonstrates how deeply patriarchal religion had taken root in her young mind (15). Unlike Firdaus's peasant father, Zahra's father was relatively educated, from an illustrious middle class family—so much so that it is one of her husband's primary reasons for marrying her. As the story progresses, al-Shaykh strips Zahra's father of his hypocrisy and the illusion of his masculine strength, unveiling the weakness of the masculine without the feminine, the patriarchal without the women to support its power structures.

Dionysus, too, has both a female and male aspect; although generally depicted only in male form, the Dionysian principle involves fertility and ecstasy, transition and transcendence. The practices devoted to this eternal principle were kept secret, but are synonymous with ritual madness and a powerful rapture that overrides ego and inhibitions, and liberates the individual from social and gendered constructs. Dionysus has dozens of epithets, amongst which are *Eleutherios*, "the Liberator," and, in keeping with the carnivalesque spirit, allows the full participation of the marginalized and abject, such as women and slaves. Like Osiris and Jesus, he is a dying and rising god. Thus, Dionysus offers another link between sex and death. In his reflections on sex and death, Osho states, "Death is encountered in meditation and death is encountered in sexual orgasm." Both religion and sex embrace death: "That blissful moment when your ego is lost and you are merged into existence is a certain death: death of the ego, death of the conscious, death of your individuality" (57). Bataille is more explicit on the connections between sex and death, "...secretly and at the deepest level the crack [death] belongs intimately to human sensuality and is the mainspring of pleasure" (105). When Zahra seeks the sniper, is she really seeking death, or fulfillment, or both? Bataille continues,

"[I]n principle eroticism seems at first sight the very opposite of this horrifying paradox. ... In fact the individual splits up and his unity is shattered from the first instant of the sexual crisis" (105). The opposing forces of sex and death, like the forces of animal urge and human restraint, form part of the tension of Zahra's being. She must destroy restraints and transgress taboos in her quest for becoming. One of her key transitions is seeking the sniper in order to offer him her body; though it may result in her immediate death, it may also result in her liberation. Through the sexually sublime experiences with the sniper ("god of death"), Zahra paradoxically reaches a part of her humanity that was closed to her before.

Zahra's earlier abject sexual experiences push her into the liminal, the ambiguous, chaotic, and in-between spaces of the grotesque sublime. Unpredictable, dangerous, and subversive, the sublime connected with sex can be rapturously transcendent. It can annihilate that which separates masculine/feminine, memory/future, reason/irrationality, life/death. It can walk tragedy "through the corridors of Pan" (Ronell xiii), perhaps the most primordial deity of all, from whom we derive the word panic. Even Pan, the ruttish goat commonly depicted with a phallus, originally celebrated a feminine aspect as an earth goddess. Again and again, Zahra comes into contact with what may be considered the dark side of the masculine sexual sublime, in which she struggles to attain a feminist consciousness or becomingness.

Zahra is rejected and othered, and even her body is othered from her being: it is a tool for others' pleasure and possession, but not her own. It is not impossible that this is entirely explained by masochistic theories, but there may be another interpretation. There is no opportunity for the self-awareness of Zahra's conscious 'I' to become integrated with her subpersonalities, which leads to her mental breakdown and hospitalization. This frustration of the Dionysian ideal is only relieved and consummated by violence and death. Feminist epistemology should perhaps try to account for the range of experiences offered by the sexual sublime in its merging or deconstruction of the dichotomies that are inherent in patriarchal thought structures.

## 3.9.2 Hysteria and depression

Zahra's uncontrollable outbursts of wild profanity, psychotic laughter, and hyperactivity mirror the stereotype of a hysterical woman. Although al-Shaykh does not employ directly mimetic methodology, she does exploit the one-dimensional quality of stereotypes of women by revealing Hashem's and Majed's self-justificatory thoughts. The ease with which they typify and pigeonhole Zahra, and exculpate themselves, explains a great deal about the walls of misunderstanding that she encounters. At the same time, al-Shaykh avoids unproblematic answers. When Zahra returns to Beirut, she is in the grip of a deep depression, but at the same time she realizes, "that I was not an easy person to cope with" (126). Her pathetically desperate sexual secrets had driven her to seek a new life in another continent, "Africa had been the shaft of a deep well down which I had hidden my threadbare secret", only to find that her uncle was unconcerned with whether or not she was a virgin upon her wedding, it was "beside the point and not worth mentioning. Educated people understood this well enough and would never dream of bringing the matter up" (126 & 112).

Surviving the new reality of war in Beirut is, at first, painless for Zahra: she is completely oblivious to the world outside. Her world is inside the house, where she never has to change from her housecoat. Her apathy, lethargy, and enclosure are complete. "My mother comes into the room and says, 'We still have a whole sack of flour. We can survive a month without needing anything else.' A month, two months, what's the difference? ..." (124).

Because of the war, Zahra can avoid life, avoid sex, and avoid normal personal and familial confrontations:

> When I heard that the battles raged fiercely and every front was an inferno, I felt calm. It meant that my perimeters were fixed by these walls, that nothing which my mother hoped for me could find a place inside them. The idea of my marrying again was buried deep by the thunder and lightning of the rockets. (126)

She no longer cares about the scabs all over her face, neck, and shoulders but recognizes that her indifference is the numbed response of one who has felt too much. Her body is important to the story on many levels, including her skin. Allen comments on the two-part structure of the novel, the war inside being symbolized by Zahra's acne, and in the second half of the novel it is replaced by the clamor, disturbance and violence outside. It is even suggested that her acne disappears as a result.

> My silence was a sickness. My mother would launch into a tirade whenever she saw me in my housecoat during those two months, but I stayed completely silent. My indifference to her anxieties, especially when she tried to get out of me my real reason for divorcing Majed, was also a sickness. (126)

She blocks herself off completely from others. After accidentally encountering her former lover Malek, she makes herself as unyielding as wood. She has sacrificed her virginity to Malek and in return received neither transcendence nor redemption. Having been brought up a Shi'ite, Zahra subscribes to or is surrounded by a belief system that especially esteems sacrifice and martyrdom—her own treatment of her sexuality suggests the strong hold that these notions have on her subconscious. She herself does not understand why she keeps sacrificing herself to Malek. The contours and rituals of grief and repentance, sacrifice and redemption that shape Shi'ite thought also affect Zahra's sexuality. Her passivity with Malek, allowing him to control her body, is her surrender to the continuation of the patriarchal order, and a form of self-punishment or atonement. She is complicit in the blood sacrifice of her virginity and her repeated abortions. She is then haunted by fear and guilt without even having first enjoyed the pleasure of sin.

## 3.10 Sacrifice

The study by Rainer Brunner and Werner Ende of modern Twelver political and religious culture notes that, "[s]uffering, sacrifice, martyrdom, and tears are, as it is well known, positive notions in popular Shi'ite belief. They are signs of honor. During the Shi'ite Passion Plays, for example, the tears of the onlookers are often collected in a sponge and revered like a reliquary" (357). Zahra's sexuality may be mingled with her death drive: she courts deadly danger when she presents her body to the sniper, and only the god of death brings her to sexual awakening. Accad equates Zahra's "death" with suicide, "since she goes to the sniper with the fear and exaltation she might be killed" (41). The voice of the narrator, which persists after the supposed death of Zahra, the character, renders the scene multilayered and ambiguous. Mbembe reminds us that, "[d]eath in the present is the mediator of redemption. Far from being an encounter with a limit, boundary, or barrier, it is experienced as a release from terror and bondage" (79).

The larger blood sacrifice that fuels patriarchal political authority, operated by the massive transnational military industrial complex and petty warlords alike, is at first Zahra's refuge and safety net.

> I felt as unyielding as wood, and stayed like that for many days, until a cease-fire was announced. Then I panicked. ... The cease-fire meant I could no longer stay in bed for hours on end, or wander aimlessly about the kitchen as the radio blared. The ceasefire meant having to leave the house. It meant going outside, and seeing people, and they seeing me for what I was. (127)

Zahra believes that the visitors who come by are only coming to observe her grotesqueness or her madness, and she refuses to engage with her environment. Her experience of the sublime is that of the transitional, the liminal, the marginalized. But

Zahra's denial of the pressures and tragedies of war begins to erode under constant news reports and the increasing proximity of the attacks. Her resolute indifference cracks as the tempo of the violence quickens, and her home is no longer a refuge. As miriam cooke explains, the war blurred the public and private, home and street, to an unprecedented extent. Ironically, the war which was intended to preserve and prolong patriarchal political power also undermined that authority, as discussed elsewhere in this study.

After an attack on their building, Zahra cries on her mother's shoulders—the violence has penetrated her world and rendered her whole family abject. Her father has changed, but it is really Zahra who has gone through sudden transition and catharsis, precipitated by terror. Abruptly, a new reality is visible to her and she now perceives him as he actually is, rather than as the relentlessly frightening monster of her childhood. A new horror has far outweighed the dread she felt towards him. "He was no longer a fat monster…. I noticed how thin his body had become, and how his head had developed a constant trembling, just like an old man who used to sit outside our school, selling yellow pulses" (138).

## 3.10.1 Subverting the order of the living and the dead

It is in the context of this new awakening that Zahra strives for subjectivity and self-realization, and she notices changes in her personality. Her *Qarina* appears[12] luring her towards sexual completion, which she does not attain. Zahra tries to ignore her unfulfilled sexuality. She felt life "start to revive" in her when she sought a sniper who lived high in the rooftops (146). It may have been her death drive, joined with her sex drive, that was activated when she took the bold step of going to him. She is the agent, actively in quest of her completion/destruction. "In that critical moment I said to myself, 'Well, here I am. I am about to lose myself for ever. Will I hear the shot first, or will I fall before I hear the shot?'" (147).

Even as she marveled that her fear had vanished, it came back in a tidal wave as she waited to be obliterated. Instead, he pounces on her and quickly takes her. The act has profound importance in Zahra's being and becoming. Anne Dufourmantelle believes that sex has been ignored by philosophical inquiry (36).

After her visit with the sniper, Zahra is as relaxed and happy as if she "had just heard the war had ended" (150). She does not herself feel pleasure, but she seems to know that he has the power to give her what she needs to complete her sexually because she is uplifted and continues to see him. In the second week of going to him, she begins to feel "a certain pleasure… Feelings of security, of comfort, even of relaxation…" until at last she is bold enough to guide him to bring her to climax (154). She undergoes a series of flashbacks of childhood traumas—seeing again her mother and a man who might be Dr Shawky, and her brutish father, as vision

---

[12] A figure of Arabic folklore, the Qarina or spirit-wife, somewhat resembles the succubus, in that it visits a sleeping person in order to have sex with the person in their dreams.

succeeds vision. She experiences something of the therapeutic arc described by Joseph Campbell in which past emotions are released and the individual's beingness evolves towards self-realization. She apprehends a series of annihilations and re-creations in her transition. She shares a revelation that it has been exhausting to be sick, and seems to come to terms with her unconscious efforts to return to the womb.

> My cries as I lay in the dust, responding to the sniper's exploring fingers, contained all the pain and sickness from my past, when I had curled up in my shell in some corner somewhere, or in a bathroom, hugging myself and holding my breath as if always trying to return to the state of being a fetus in its mother's womb. (154)

Zahra undergoes a Dionysian sublime, in which the chaos of sex, life and death merge. Ultimately, as Nietzsche suggests, the Dionysian ecstasy must lead to tragedy, because only in tragedy can one fully attain the Dionysian sublime (26–27, 36, 50). Zahra is liberated from floods of raw emotion and painful memories. She finally understands what happened to her in Africa and her hospitalization, as her non-being seems to shift into being and becoming.

> Crying out, lying on dusty floor tiles in an abandoned building, breathing the air's fear and sadness, my lord and master a god of death who had succeeded in making my body tremble with ecstasy for the first time in thirty years. My body had undulated with pleasure as the sniper looked into my eyes. (154)

He seems to have returned her gaze. Is it the first time someone has really looked into her eyes? Eyes, the windows to the soul, are also the soul's window to the world. But her eyes only really open for the first time as she lies bleeding on the street. Mbembe states that, "For man to reveal himself in the end, he has to die, but he will have to do so while alive—by looking at himself ceasing to exist" (12). There is little or nothing of the overtly metaphysical about *The Story of Zahra*; it remains delicately nuanced and uncertain. If the sniper has killed her, Zahra's end may be interpreted as the simple biological cessation of life and nothing more. This does not seem entirely satisfactory from a number of perspectives. At times, Zahra resorts to prayer, but she does not discuss religion much, and it may be inferred that she is not very religious. However, given her religio-cultural environment and her own sacrificial death drive, it seems unlikely that she herself would have viewed her life and death as being devoid of deeper spiritual meaning. In *The Invention of Dionysus: An Essay on The Birth of Tragedy*, James Porter presents Nietzsche's own contradictory views on metaphysics, which may well reflect that of many modern Western thinkers (19).

Humans have not yet outgrown their need for assigning meaning, especially to those events that touch the realm of mystery, such as sex and death. And Zahra has attained transcendence of some kind, however it may be interpreted. Bataille wrote of the role of anguish in the sublime: "Anguish always works in the same way. The greatest anguish, the anguish in the face of death, is what men desire in order to transcend it beyond death and ruination" (87). In his own way, Bataille highlights the importance of overcoming the self/other duality. Humans are discontinuous beings, seeking to become continuous, which they experience transiently with eroticism and lastingly in death. In her musings on sex and philosophy, and the self/other dichotomy, Anne Dufourmantelle writes, "Philosophy is a language for coming to terms with the foreign body that I call 'you,' the plural world that persists in being other than itself, the language that makes beings of words and desire" (32).

Sex can speak the language of philosophy, if we have the ears to listen. Al-Shaykh unsilences the thought-provoking aspects of sex and being, and sweeps away what Avital Ronell calls "oblitature," or the "space of thinking's disavowal." Ronell's explanation of the "Dionysian pulse" that has been felt for thousands of years also partly explains al-Shaykh's achievement in harnessing the ancient bisexual power of Dionysus in the service of modern feminist explorations of identity, being, and sexuality through the sublime (xiii - xiv).

Whether darkened under censorship or "whited out by the blinding light of surveillance", sex and truth are misrepresented and concealed (Ronell xviii). Nietzsche wondered if, "Socratic morality, dialectic, the satisfaction and serenity of the theoretical man" destroyed the Dionysian *jouissance*; he asked if such seeming serenity was, in fact, "a sign of collapse, exhaustion, sickness, the anarchic dissolution of the instincts" (3). His uncompromising view that morality destroys art is borne out if we understand morality to mean the repressive morality that judges others, suppresses narratives such as *The Story of Zahra* and renders the story impossible to understand. Al-Shaykh's work is ill-served by such morality, which is entirely irrelevant to productive engagement with the other, the liminal zone of the hybrid, with anarchy, excess, the hidden and forbidden. The Dionysian must be balanced with the Apollonian in order to be truly effective and sustainable, just as other dichotomies must be merged, deconstructed, or transcended. *Logos* needs chaos for its proper development. One of the accomplishments of *The Story of Zahra* is the revival of the philosophical beauty and value of chaos.

## 3.10.2 Blood, sex and death

For Zahra, sex is a sacrifice without the sacrament and without redemption. She sacrifices her virginity and then repeatedly gives herself to Malek without joy or pleasure. Her relationship with the sniper is complex, and strongly suggests the quest for forbidden knowledge, liberation and ontopoiesis in the sublime.

Unlike Firdaus, Zahra's body has not been surgically mutilated but Zahra's disassociation from her body and her lack of ownership of her embodied Self renders her body almost a foreign object to be despised, disfigured, subjugated. Firdaus, on the other hand, was cut off from one of the body parts that made up her womanliness and her ability to experience transcendent pleasure. The clitoris is unique to women as a body part devoted exclusively to pleasure—evidently, it serves no other function. The male body lacks a feature dedicated to pleasure, as the penis is multi-purposed. Some cultures acknowledged women's superiority in being able to achieve the sublime through sex, partly because her physical make up is better suited to repeated orgasm. The pre-Islamic practice of female genital mutilation may spring from the fear of empowered, subjectified women. Jonathan Margolis explains that:

> [M]any ancient cultures believed their orgasms were mystical experiences, ... It should be of no wonder, really, that the rapturous sensation of the immediate aftermath of orgasm was revered as something on a parallel with a religious experience. (43)

Firdaus's body was mutilated, and she was thereby denied the opportunity to experience the sexual sublime, in contrast, Zahra was psychologically maimed and unable to exert ownership over her body or to take pleasure in it.

Without a space to experience, let alone assert, her subjectivity, Zahra is merely existing or surviving. She desperately wants to attain that realized, reflective self-awareness which leads to becomingness. On a more basic level, she wants to repudiate others' ownership, and simply be able to own herself, her body and her mind. "I wanted to live for myself. I wanted my body to be mine alone. I wanted the place on which I stood and the air surrounding me to be mine alone and no one else's" (al-Shaykh 93). But she seems to have no means to bring about this end, and she is forced to take drastic measures in order to bring about her subjectivity.

Victor Turner's description of the liminoid as simultaneously negative and possessed of infinite potential helps to illuminate Zahra's quest for eroticism. The sacrificial logic of sex could be pivotal in the transitions Zahra's liminal being must undergo to realize full subjectivity as a woman. Liminality is the zero, while eroticism is the affirmative and decisive. (cf. Turner 97 on liminality). Zahra is sexually active, yet in a way that gives only anguish, shame, and fear of discovery. Unable to achieve orgasm and denied one of the sublime experiences, Zahra is almost asexual—certainly, her sexual experiences are not erotic. She has an uneasy relationship with her body and everyone and everything in her environment—she cannot remember a time when she was not uneasy (al-Shaykh 111).

Zahra's relationship with Malek is excessive, grotesque and abject all at once. As though punishing her body, she gives him her body over and over, without any real participation, wondering why she keeps coming to him. She repeats her mother's pattern of abortions, resorting to two abortions and surgically restoring her virginity to give transient pleasure to a man who does not even pretend to love her or respect her. This strangely joyless relationship between Malek and Zahra reflects her discomfort with and rejection of her own body and her own Being. She is disassociated, a potentially dangerous psychological condition, and submits unwillingly to the dominant male. She wonders at and rails against her own docility and submissiveness, which is so strongly inculcated in her that it leads to excess. In *Patterns in Comparative Religion*, Mircea Eliade, points out, "excesses fulfill a definite and useful role in the economy of the sacred. They break down the barriers between man, society, nature and the gods" (21). The excess of genuine eroticism and pleasure is denied to Zahra; instead, she indulges in an excess of abjection, self-disfigurement, self-hatred. She does not seem to believe that she owns her body, and perhaps she factually does not. Her parents, her husband, her lovers, exert ownership over her that supersedes her own will. She is out of touch with her body; it is as though it belongs to someone else. She is frustrated at every level—physical, mental, spiritual. She laments, "I am at my wits' end, and am annoyed with myself and hate myself because I stay silent. When will my soul cry out like a woman surrendering to a redeeming love?" (34). She desires the "assent to life up to the point of death," as Bataille says to distinguishes eroticism from the instinct or will to reproduce; both, however, are intricately linked with death.

Zahra reaches the sublime through sex only with her lover, a god of death. Perhaps significantly, she achieves her first orgasm not through penetration but through his fingers—she has already been serially, repeatedly violated by penetration. This is the sublime that breaks down barriers, evokes and discharges the pain in her past memories, liberates and destroys her. But to break free from her emotional shell, she must first break free from the bonds of fear.

Zahra is driven by fear, after having been repeatedly terrorized in her early life, chiefly by a violent father. She held him in dread and genuine fear for her life—one of her childhood memories of her father beating her to force a confession about her mother's infidelities caused her such fear that she urinated where she stood. Fear is all around her: fear of her father's lashing tongue and leather belt; fear of strangers mocking her; fear of not fitting in with society; fear of people finding out what she really is; fear of rockets and bullets; fear of death. She has become pathologically inhibited, passive, unable to express herself, even to herself. In any context, the act of approaching a stranger whom one believes to be a sniper who kills at random is bold. In the context of Zahra's fearfulness, the act is extreme. One explanation is that her death drive and sex drive are perversely linked. She is on the verge of the sexual sublime—as her encounter with her Qarina demonstrates—and she now seeks the ultimate sacrifice, as part of her ultimate fulfillment. In keeping with this perversity, as she draws near the place she believes the sniper is located, her fears drop away from her even as she fully expects to encounter death. "Well, here I am. I am about to lose myself for ever. Will I hear the shot first, or will I fall before I hear the shot?" (147). Fear and dread are amongst the primary components of the sublime. Zahra has inhabited the liminal space of hysteria, alienation, and psychosis, staring into the void for so long that she has come through her fears to find some sort of balance at another level of consciousness. Her transition through fear is an important step on her path. Although the liminal place is both everywhere and nowhere, traditionally, doorways and crossroads may represent the edges of the liminal. Zahra has stepped out of the formless and shifting liminal, and chosen a fork in the road onto a definite path.

## 3.11 Destruction as the origin of becoming

Zahra is overwhelmed with the forcefulness of sudden fear, which disappears at the sound of the sniper's voice. The intensity of such experiences may put them on par with one of the emblematic liminal experiences: the near-death incident. Is Zahra deliberately courting excessive danger in the subconscious hope of a near-death transformation? She seems to be both attracted to and repelled by death.

Whether Zahra has undergone what may be called a near-death experience is arguable, but not untenable. Mary Ann Kenney's study of the phenomenology of personal transformation includes the near-death experience through illness and accident; Zahra's shattering breakdowns, and now her proximity to death through war suggest the metamorphic potential of harrowing confrontations with death.

Kenney cites Jung on his own brush with death: "I no longer attempted to put across my own opinion, but surrendered myself to the current of my thoughts" (8). While he is simply recounting his own experience and makes no claim for its universality, the change exemplified by his acceptance of the uncertainty of his destiny, his essential acceptance of death, is reflected in others' accounts of near-death experiences.

Kenney cites Walton's phenomenological research, in which he interviews people who had reached points in their lives where they were feeling stagnation, loss and desperation. Their incidents approaching death were "like bottoming out for an addict"; they suddenly had the energy to revolutionize their lives (9). Interpreted in this light, it could be said that Zahra has bottomed out and is actively seeking transformation. Having already occupied the liminal, the marginal and the inferior—the three manifestations of human interrelationships identified by Victor Turner—she has nowhere else to go. Turner has said that liminal individuals are, "neither here nor there; they are betwixt and between the positions assigned and arrayed by law, custom, convention, and ceremony" (95). Zahra is nothing and nowhere; she has no place to *be*, in the fullest sense of the word, and she has nothing of her own, not even her body. Turner stresses that liminal individuals have nothing: "no status, insignia, secular clothing, rank, kinship position, nothing to demarcate them structurally from their fellows" (98). Zahra, like Firdaus, is at point zero. However, as we have seen, zero is both nothing and everything. Zero is not just "nil"— zero can misbehave, transgress, and upend the dominant order. By reaching bottom, Zahra may be able to reach the top. The flip side of being "betwixt and between" is what Turner calls the "realm of pure possibility." But however strong Zahra's drive towards the realization of her subjectivity and possibilities may be, she is burdened with a past that constricts her like a straightjacket.

At an early age, Zahra was suborned to perjury by a mother who does not even share the camaraderie of being an accomplice in infidelity with her daughter—her mother's denial is complete. Her mother mocks and ridicules her, her father harshly belittles her. Zahra's relationship with her parents is unaffectionate, invalidative, and distressing. Her escape from her family (and inability to marry locally) to wedlock in Africa was to enmesh her more deeply with her internal demons. Her awareness of being aware was so disturbed that it is hard to discern what she does and does not know at the time of her breakdown. Whether she internalizes her stay in the mental hospital as a near-death experience is questionable but seems unlikely. She only comes to understand what happened then much later, when she is shuddering in the arms of the god of death, annihilating her past traumas, fear, and inhibitions, her former Self.

## 3.11.1 Near-death and the sublime

Thanatos (Death) is often depicted as the opposite of Eros. But opposites meet somewhere. In the introduction to *Death and Sensuality,* Georges Bataille writes, "I do not seek to identify them with each other but I endeavour to find the point where they may converge beyond their mutual exclusiveness" (7). In *The Story of Zahra*, the opposing forces of sex and death perform an uneasy balancing act, a harmonious dance of such fragility that the harmony can be marred at any moment. Although Zahra approaches a man, a stranger, to give herself to him and put her body at his disposal, she may be seeking death or near-death in an impersonal, symbolic manner. Death may be regarded on different levels—the birth of her new Self must be accompanied by the death of her old Self. Death can be symbolically conceptualized (as by Jung and Assagioli) as the mediator between different levels of consciousness, as subpersonalities become integrated into the conscious, in the evolution towards the superconscious. Zahra seldom speaks to the personification of death that she has purposefully sought: "Then, to my surprise, I heard him speak my name. I had given him my body, my chance of life or death, but never my name" (152). Did she reserve some part of herself from him, in the irrational hope that his power over her would be less if he did not know her name, if she remained anonymous? The power of the knowing a name is well known in religion and folklore, and beliefs connected with knowledge and naming are current in the Middle East. Yet she tells her aunt that the sniper kills at random, and her great fear of him after she left him indicates that, on an emotional level at least, she understands that she has transgressed boundaries into the realm of death.

> As I ran down the stairs I cursed my fear. In the street I held close to the walls. I thought of how one of his bullets could now kill his secret and me with it, even as I also told myself that he couldn't possibly have doubts about me, else why had he let me go? But then I kept wondering .... (160)

Zahra's justification for seeking the sniper—that she can perhaps startle him into ceasing to kill—seems improbable, and indeed, when she does meet him, she makes no attempt to dissuade him from spilling innocent blood, and soon abandons that idea. "What should I have done, I wondered? I had lost a rare chance, briefly meeting a sniper feared by the community when he was not holding his rifle. …I should have asked him to lay down his arms. Yet such thoughts soon faded" (160). Her rationalization for seducing Death himself is an invention to obscure her actual motivation from her conscious awareness. Just as the war has brought her new energy, so does flirting with death bring her to the land of the living. Perhaps this paradox is best summated in Mary Ann Kenney's study of personal transformation, citing Trappey's research into near-death experiences, in which she suggests that, "destruction is the origin of becoming…What appears to be destroyed is actually in the process of becoming" (153). Zahra is on the cusp of discovering her own being, and enabling her becoming.

Zahra's shocking encounters with death and violence through the war have caused her own problems to shrink in comparison. Images of bodies torn apart, bodies mixed with shrapnel, bodies that, an instant ago were a family playing cards in their living room, have invaded her daily consciousness:

> At that point my father's image came into my mind, shrunken, lacking the Hitler-like moustache and with no watch in his trouser pocket. By now his heavy frame had lost all sign of the brute strength with which he had beaten my mother. His voice no longer carried a threat of thunder. (152)

The imminence of death—sudden, senseless death—has forced Zahra to reposition herself in her environment, and quickly to discover and develop her subjectivity. The keen awareness of life's fragility is the essence of the near-death experience that precipitates transitions and metamorphosis. Mary Ann Kenney's research into the near-death incident (or series of incidents) as a chrysalis cites numerous studies: "All of the people who were interviewed experienced a spiritual and emotional transformation" (168). They "viewed their near-death experience as a pivotal force in helping them make [personal changes]" (178). Moreover, Kenney cites Trappey's phenomenological study of people who had come close to death through illness. Trappey states, "[a]ll the participants dissolved psychologically during their near-death experience" (153). Dissolution is also intimately involved in eroticism. Bataille explains his views on the dissolution of discontinuity, and states that, "The whole business of eroticism is to destroy the self-contained character of the participants as they are in their normal lives" (17).

Zahra's discontinuity is unbearable to her, and she urgently needs to dissolve the psychological web that has held her relentlessly since childhood. Her struggles to loosen the strings of the web have resulted in entrapping her further and more deeply;

her only escape is through knowledge, which is reached through the overwhelming forces of sex, death, and sacrifice.

Zahra deliberately intensifies the near-death experience that is wartime by courting extreme danger and Death himself in the person of the sniper. She takes a role that is both active and submissive:

> As the sniper drew me closer, I was totally submissive. He spread me out in the narrow space in front of the doors that led out on to the roof, lifted my skirt with one hand as the fingers of his other secretly explored between my thighs. .... And whenever his hand seemed about to depart, I would tense my thighs together and urge it back into its trap. (152)

Thus, she has already changed to the point that she can take some measure of control; she guides him and insisted that he bring her to her first-ever orgasm. This "little death" is also her rebirth. It is said that death started with sex.

William R. Clark's *Sex and the Origins of Death* traces the evolutionary beginning of death to the point at which sex is introduced. Simple organisms that do not reproduce sexually do not die; on a fundamental physical level, sex and death are interrelated and inextricably linked. So, too, they are related psychologically, symbolically, religiously, culturally.

Clark (ix) echoes Heidegger, who understands the acceptance or overcoming of the terror and fascination of impending death as part of a higher form of Being. Death plays a powerful role in Zahra's being as she consciously or unconsciously seeks the knowledge of herself, and the highest mode of being-towards-death. Clark goes on to describe cellular death and, in the case of asexual reproduction, immortality. In short, death, suicide and even endless life are variously programmed into different types of cells. In *Sex and Death, An Introduction to Philosophy of Biology*, Kim Sterelny and Paul E. Griffiths propose philosophical, psychological and sociological theories derived from biological facts. They note that while the facts may be indisputable, the philosophies based on those facts are not, stripping the aura of scientific invincibility from numerous cherished (mis)conceptions. Viewing Zahra's behavior in light of an evolutionary mandate may be attractive, but such a framework is no more inherently scientific than the contributions to human thought given us by Heidegger, Foucault, or Henry Corbin.

## 3.11.2 Denying the death drive

Zahra pretends that the sniper might not be a sniper, that he might actually marry her. She actually knows what he is—denying his true being is repudiating part of her own nature, denying that she needed sacrifice, death and near-death to come to life. Is she fooling herself, or her reader, or both? Denying the tension and dissonance that sustained their rather complex relationship has the effect of nullifying it.

The union between Zahra and the sniper who may or may not be named Sami is intense but also impersonal, and is fraught with the unspoken. miriam cooke writes of the Lebanese war, "Such an atmosphere assumed the loss of dialogue…In such an atmosphere, compromise and communication were no longer possible" (9). This environment, combined with Zahra's own inhibitions, seems to render her mostly silent when she is with the sniper. She listens to his stories, but contributes little to the one-sided conversations. She retains her opacity and is closed to him, even while opening to receive him sexually. He, too, remains mysterious. He disappears without word to her during the time of a truce, and returns upon the resumption of hostilities. Yet she tries to convince herself that he is a man like any other, and that there could be a future with him. Her excursion into this self-constructed fantasy is fatal. Her narrative is imbued with what cooke calls the "incarnation of tragic awareness" (10).

When she pretends that the sniper is not a sniper, she debates within herself and admits that he must be: "Of course he is a sniper, the freebooter captain of a leaky pirate ship that sails through this war's contradictions and has taken me on board" (173). Her vacillation about his status as a man or a god of death reflects her own disassociation with or denial of the enormity of what she has done in going to him in the first place, and what she does in going to him daily. It also mirrors her life-long pattern of ambiguity as a way to negotiate the dictatorial oppositional binaries in her patriarchal environment.

Having experienced the world outside, she cannot return to the womblike safety of the bathroom. She is transitioning, and even as her awareness is developing, the imperative of Being does not allow her to revert to a fetal position, cut off from all human contact. She embraces the confusion, not knowing, and powerlessness of her in-betweenness as a tool to uncover the deeper truth and reality of being.

> I just want to stay in this house. If the bathroom had a lock, I would make that my home. But no, I know I will continue to see him every day, to experience that confusion and fear as my feet barely touch the ground or the stair tiles; will know the smell of his sweat, his piercing eyes, my arms gripping his back, making him bear down on me with his full weight. Ah, the beautiful numbness which I feel after I come. For a few moments it plunges me into total darkness. His closed eyes never witness my ecstasy. Yet I myself cannot fully absorb the intensity of those long moments. …I forget I have ever promised myself never to return, even as I forget my decision to stop at home and never answer the door. (173)

Burke describes the sublime as "the precipitation beyond oneself", and Heidegger specifically places the "ecstasy or ravishment" as beyond anxieties; in her encounters with the sniper, Zahra is released from the fear that has ruled her life (48). Even if the release is only momentary, it has forever changed her view of herself, her autonomy, her subjectivity. Having been stretched, her mind cannot now go back to quite the same shape.

She seems to repudiate the paradox of her own sexuality and death drive when she asks him if he is a sniper. His outraged, passionately angry response is revealing, but she does not need that revelation. She already knows. So why does she ask him? Is she testing him, tempting him to do what he has failed to do before, when he has surprisingly refused to kill her? She admits her conscious duplicity, when she asks herself if he will continue to tell her lies. "Can he be a sniper? I must leave all my anxiety and questioning behind. Once we are married, he will, if he is a sniper, ask to be moved to some other duty. Or will he continue to tell me lies whenever he sets out from the house?" (213). The question of how aware she is of the death-driven and sacrificial character of her sexuality is open to interpretation.

Alan Watts posits the sacrifice inherent to the male/female relationship, using an analysis of Genesis which highlights Adam's androgyny and forgetfulness of his/her original, native identity as "a further extension of the sacrificial character of the creation, as when an actor, playing a part, forgets his proper identity and identifies himself with the persona he has assumed" (52). Adam has lost his/her spiritual awakeness and thereby, "substantial unity with God." Watts goes on the demonstrate that "the Fall is the subordination of the human mind to the dualistic predicament" and that the opposition of male/female indicates "duality rather than sexuality" (52). Blurring the boundaries of being, Zahra's shift from the marginalized, inferior and liminoid to Being-toward-death could be activated by the profound human need to explore and transcend the "dualistic predicament" of male/female. Bataille evokes fundamental connections between sex, death, and sacrifice. He relies on the concept of the discontinuousness of beings, our essential separateness and aloneness, and desire for continuousness, to explain the underpinnings of eroticism and sacrifice: "What I want to emphasize is that death does not affect the continuity of existence … continuity of existence is independent of death and is even proved by death" (22). The ending of her story, if it is the end, is also a continuousness. She seems to have transcended death. The nature of that transcendence is open to interpretation. Bataille further sheds light on the relationship between religion, death, sacrifice and eroticism, which have the "revelation of continuity" in common (22).

Whether ultimately to transcend mortality, or to end in the nothingness of non-being, Zahra seems to propel herself towards death. She experiences the fleeting pain and joy of the dissolution of self as a discontinuous being, unveiling the hidden and creating new awareness. The sniper penetrates her impregnable emotional armor but impregnates her body. Had she not been seeking death on some level, she might have considered leaving. She seems unaware that gods of death (Osiris, Thanatos, Pluto, etc.) cannot have children.

Zahra utters the unutterable. Knowing the answer, she asks him if he is a sniper. "I have only whispered, in case the walls should hear, but he stands up abruptly, crazy with bitterness, formidable in his anger, and shouts out, 'Sniper? What do you say? You really must be insane! Do you distrust me to that extent?'..." and he resorts to telling her what she knows are lies (210). By telling him she is pregnant and voicing what has always been unsaid, she both reveals truth and obscures it. The truth that she needs him to further her being-towards-death imperative and that he serves as a tool to bring about her inner change, is obscured by her desire to personalize him, to tame and domesticate the forces of sex, sacrifice and death.

### 3.11.3 Culmination of the Dionysian ideal

His impending betrayal is clearly, ironically marked by his use of the word trust. "He nods as if he has just awakened and speaks dreamily, 'Don't worry. Trust me!'" (212). When she is walking home, she feels the first two bullets, and temporality is suspended: "the whole of my past and present runs together" (214). Her eyes meet darkness. Although it is dark, the skies turn white. "As I close my eyes for an instant I see the stars of pain. Then there are rainbows arching across white skies. He kills me. He kills me with the bullets that lay at his elbow as he made love to me" (215).

Just how reliable is Zahra as a narrator? Does she experience a meeting with something beyond herself, a dimension of Dasein that transcends physical death, what Corbin terms Being-beyond-Death? "The rainbows still arch in the white skies. Rainbow follows rainbow. Sky follows sky. Rainbows of brilliant color pursue each other across skies of blinding whiteness." Her penultimate sentence is perhaps the most important in her entire story: "I close my eyes that perhaps were never truly opened." She has urgently struggled to achieve critical self-awareness and full subjectivity as a woman. If blood and sacrifice are the necessary price for knowledge, she has paid. While there can be little doubt that she has progressed towards her goal, we cannot be sure that she has achieved it. If tragedy is the highest culmination of the Dionysian ideal, she may well have achieved it.

*The Story of Zahra* resists straightforward analysis and easy answers. It raises contradictions that cannot be resolved. In awakening, and overcoming what miriam cooke describes as the "numbed condition of passivity" (11) during wartime, Zahra risks her very being in the process of becoming. Zahra's mind is at odds with itself. The war is both internal and external. This strife "does not work toward resolution but toward a preservation of difference and opposition—an en-countering—in thought" (10), which is described by Alan Milchman and Alan Rosenberg in the context of dealing with conflicting thought, *Auseinandersetzung*, "separate ways of thinking belong together in their opposition and difference" (10).

The gathering of disparate realities is one of the hallmarks of *The Story of Zahra*. Rather than a Roshomon-like postmodernist reflection on differing subjective truths that render an objective truth impossible, al-Shaykh has given us the luxury of not knowing, ambiguity as a form of resistance to patriarchal dichotomies, allowing multiple, simultaneous ways to perceive ourselves and others. In Zahra's own words, "Let us open ourselves to accept the unknown, whatever it may bring" (138).

## 4  NIGHT OF THE FIRST BILLION

Like *The Story of Zahra*, *Night of the First Billion* centers on the Lebanese civil war, but the action is almost entirely set in Switzerland. The opening is a mysterious but evocative and meaningful incantation, invoking divine light, the subjugation of demons and the kings of the jinn, casting out evil spirits, and the acquisition of glittering jewels, pearls and rare wisdom. The action shifts abruptly. A harrowing, hairsbreadth escape from Beirut at the time of the Israeli invasion is followed by the luxury of a hotel by Lac Leman. Kafa has been planning this escape for seven years, while her husband Khalil fought for what he believed to be right. After the death of their daughter, Widad, Kafa went into deep mourning and became estranged from her husband. Yet in their new environment, so serene and beautiful, the tragedy of the war is not over, and Kafa and Khalil are not reconciled. She has saved enough money for their sons to go to private school for a few months, and Khalil feels acutely that he is penniless and out of place next to Kafa. She is still beautiful and stylish, and before she even arrives in Geneva—while still on the airplane—she is already becoming more enmeshed in materialism and aware of her feminine charms. In Geneva, the power structure and class, gender, and sociopolitical divisions of Beirut are re-enacted, and the safety of the West is exposed as an illusion.

Kafa meets Nadim Ghafir on the flight to Geneva, a rich and powerful man who is attracted to her. While she is silently sending Nadim "siren signals", Khalil is also noticing Nadim, a man "who would sell anything: arms, women, nations, planes, petrol…" (19). While Kafa is thinking about how agreeable first-class is, because the rich people who sit in first class are so refined, Khalil is thinking that he loathes the very same kind of people who take first-class. There are many such shifts of voice throughout the narrative. Nadim is the henchman of Raghid Bey Zahran, an enormously wealthy arms dealer who is obsessed with gold. Raghid is one of the chief engineers in a web of corruption which spreads from Lebanon to Switzerland. He also employs Sheikh Watfan, the sorcerer who performs the incantation at the beginning of the story, in order to control people, destroy his enemies and predict the future.

Dunya, the wife of Nadim Ghafir, enjoys an elevated social position and wealth, but is aware of the hypocrisy and emptiness of her life. She despises her husband's friends, even while entertaining them charmingly. She has been unfaithful to Nadim with his employer Raghid, and is drinking alcohol to excess, and secretly visiting Sheikh Watfan, but lacks the strength to leave the husband she dislikes. In one of many intricate political that twists mirror the hopes and dangerous betrayals at home in Lebanon, Dunya begins to be seen publicly with Amir Nealy, an enemy of Raghid's.

Raghid's duplicities seem to reflect the internecine nature of the war in Lebanon, in which there are not just two, but rather many, many sides—comrade against comrade. There are direct and indirect references to the war from differing points of view. Raghid's profiteering cynicism, for example, is contrasted with Khalil's innocence and sincerity. In a memorable scene, Khalil is forcibly drugged and made to witness a "circus." The bizarre and fantastic acts performed by the players are plainly intended to represent the insanity of the civil war--the cruelty, treachery, gender and class inequality, and the perversion of morality. Frequent references to endless nightmares and the surreal, magical, and hallucinatory are all woven into the text, thus connecting this novel with the author's two earlier works concerning the war, *Beirut '75* (1974) and *Beirut Nightmares* (1977).

The night of the first billion refers to a party, one where some 300 millionaires have been invited to Raghid's home in order to celebrate the achievement of his first billion in money. In comparison with his wealth, the millionaires are as nothing. For different characters the event has diverse meanings. For Raghid, the intention is to demonstrate his power as ostentatiously as possible. Even the tableware is gold. The garden is to be recreated as a paradise with artificial rivers of milk and honey. It is his coronation. For Kafa, it is a night when she can display her most beautiful dress and jewels, and perhaps ensnare a millionaire. For the woman whom Raghid is using both for sex and as organizer of the party, it is a chance to make an immense profit and consolidate her position socially. For the guests, it is an opportunity to make deals; "…they're attending it the way they might go to a conference for the exchange of mutual interests" (497).

There are numerous characters in the novel, but Kafa is the one in which this study takes the most interest; she is a character who undergoes transitions through the sublime which are different from, yet in some ways comparable to, those of Firdaus and Zahra. After Widad's death, she cannot go on with life as it was; she has had enough misery and constant, daily fear of death. With the change of location to Switzerland, to achieve which she sacrificed everything she owned, she still cannot obtain relief from her pain. She seeks solace from her agony in wealth, which is her only comfort. She takes on more and more lovers, and seems to become a new woman. Masculine admiration and gifts such as a magnificent sapphire Cartier necklace numb her pain and sedate her. However, the man who has given her the necklace has raped her. Her husband, who has witnessed some of that violence, has blamed her for flirting with the man. She sleeps with Raghid, which proves to be a degrading experience, partly because he gives her a ring set with a fake diamond. Not unlike Firdaus's experience, all men become one and the same man. Men and money help her to forget "Wadid, Beirut, the shattered glass, the hunger, sleeping on the floors of cockroach- and mice-infested bomb-shelters…the anticipation of the next assault by armed vigilantes" (499). Her son, Rami, will only grow up to join the militia and be killed. Eventually her despair is so deep that she leaves her husband and two sons, Rami and Fadi. She chooses socio-cultural death: she becomes a prostitute.

Interestingly, Faith Cowling points out that al-Sammān may have experienced some of the emotional and social isolation that Kafa felt. "She [al-Sammān] is quoted in Ghalia Shukri's book, *Ghada al-Sammān Bi-la Ajniha*, (Ghada Samman without wings) as saying: 'The hardest lesson I learned was my final discovery of the superficiality of the bourgeois Damascene society that used to consider me during those years as good as dead – "a fallen woman" – whereas I was in reality a woman starting to live her life and an artist gaining in awareness'" (n.pag.). As if to reflect such sentiments, *Night of the First Billion* parodies the bourgeoisie, their aspirations, and the opportunist capitalism that forms some of their financial infrastructure.

## 4.1 Irony and ambivalence

In this chapter, we will first address irony, parody and satire generally and as they relate to the feminist sublime. We will then examine al-Sammān's *Night of the First Billion* in detail. The three novels under discussion provide an interesting contrast in the use of irony to foreground transition and the sublime. All three use irony, but with very different textures and flavors. In *Woman at Point Zero* the tone of Firdaus's stoicism and her rage towards men almost precludes irony; her fierce anger is a sledgehammer, while irony is a subtler weapon. However, al-Saʿdāwī does employ irony, particularly situational irony, as when Firdaus discovers that being a respectable office worker does not much differ from being a prostitute, except in being less lucrative. Al-Saʿdāwī uses Firdaus's wide-eyed naiveté to radically defamiliarize everyday assumptions and force readers to re-evaluate their own world views. Nancy A. Walker, in her essay on the feminist use of irony and fantasy in modern novels, notes that "fantasy may be a way of constructing an unreal world from the specifics of the real, so irony is a way of negating the truth" (21).

Al-Shaykh's irony is more subtle and perhaps more thought-provokingly subversive than that of al-Saʿdāwī, but it is recognizable in her contrasting narratives—Zahra's uncle's view of himself and his own conduct has ironic elements, for example, compared with Zahra's view of the same situation and relationship. The divergent views as to what constitutes the "truth" may be ironic at times. In his essay on the Rashomon effect, Karl Heider cites Robert Redfield: "Each account, if it preserves the human quality at all, is a created product in which the human qualities of the creator in the outside viewer and describer are one ingredient" (74). Al-Shaykh preserves such human qualities in the narratives that she constructs by rejecting logical positivism and empirical understanding in favor of what Karl Heider terms "subjective metaphysical meaning-dependence" (73). The field of irony in *The Story of Zahra* lies between those opposites and in the interplay between different realities. Nancy Walker points out that irony involves the reader in the construction of meaning, thus the reader is rendered more intimately aware of and complicit in Zahra's shifting beingness, her loss of the sense of linear temporality, and splintered realities (25). In *Night of the First Billion*, as well as the two earlier works in al-Sammān's Beirut trilogy, irony is a prominent tool to disturb, question, and leave contradictions unresolved. We will briefly examine some of the tools of al-Sammān's resistance: irony; satire; and parody, with an emphasis on irony.

### 4.1.1 Irony and the feminist sublime

In Muḥsin Jāsim al- Mūsawī's work on the post-colonial Arabic novel, he points to the parallels between irony and the carnivalesque, when they are situated in opposition to hierarchical and authoritarian systems (288). Al-Mūsawī notes that laughter "wrecks" the serious, and cites Bakhtin: "Everything serious had to have, and indeed did have, its comic double" (289). This doubling construct, or symmetrical composition, is a subtle but noticeable feature in *Night of the First Billion*. Al- Mūsawī seems to make little or no distinction between irony, parody, satire, and travesty, and indeed, in many works all these components are prominent, but each element has its own characteristics. Walker pays special attention to feminist authors, and cites Lilian R. Furst about the role of irony in women's writing: "It is an inquiring mode that exploits discrepancies, challenges assumptions and reflects equivocations, but that does not presume to hold out answers" (23). Irony creates ambivalence, an important aspect of the confrontation with the sublime. Irony is so prevalent in women's writing that Walker conceives of it as "gender-specific resistance to the status quo of oppression," and highlights it as the pre-eminent mode for "expressing the flux and uncertainty of those who envision a new but indefinite social order" (22). Al-Sammān is perhaps the foremost exponent of irony amongst modern Arabic women writers.

Mastery of the force of language is necessary for irony to engage the reader in the complex web of realities spun by al-Sammān's pen. Indeed, the sorcerer's spells in *Night of the First Billion* overtly reinforce the power of words—the right words. How the right words spoken at the right time may create irony and sublimity is a point of some contention, which closely relates to al-Sammān's writing style.

### 4.1.2 Is irony incompatible with sublimity?

Longinus (or more properly, pseudo-Longinus), praises glorious language that elevates the spirit. He admires Hyperides's employment of irony and satire for the ability of those tools to disarm his opponents' arguments by making light of them (66). His concept of the sublime does not seem, therefore, entirely to preclude irony. Irony is somewhat hard to reconcile with the classical and neoclassical notions of the transcendent sublime, however. Peter Cochran gives one definition of the sublime, which is, "that before which ironical laughter is impossible" (221). He proposes irony as a useful "brake or corrective" to the danger of losing oneself in the sublime, suggesting that the two are incompatible. Al-Sammān seems, however, to manage the contradictory combination of both ironic laughter and the sublime.

Two works may help to shed some light in the evaluation of whether the sublime and the ironic can be reconciled and work together. The first is Lord Byron's *Don Juan* (1819) and the second Nabokov's *Invitation to a Beheading* (1935). The choice of these two very different pieces of writing is based simply on the fact that they may be considered excellent exemplars. Peter Cochran's study on sublimity cites Francis Cohen on *Don Juan,* a poem widely considered to be unpublishable at the time. On the very day of its release, Francis Cohen composed a critique of *Don Juan* in which he disapproved of the poet's mixing the exalted and the base in the same breath, rather than alternating between the two (225).

The irony created by the fusion of incompatible moods dampens the soaring heights of the sublime, in Cohen's opinion. Peter Cochran explains the view that, "[s]ublimity and merriment, that which is grave and that which is gay, freezing and burning, scorching and drenching, cannot… exist on the same spot. Such things may be in a poem in sequence, but not at the same time" (225). Merriment may undermine sublimity, but it also has the perverse power to destabilize authority and create space for the feminist sublime. Not as unbridled as the carnivalesque, laughter nonetheless transgresses borders or—what may be worse for authoritarian and patriarchal systems—makes light of them. Ironic laughter is disruptive, and is, perhaps, the finest form of sabotage, since it renders disciplinary figures even more ridiculous when they try to punish those who laugh at them. Al-Sammān takes on matters such as corruption, the arms industry, and myriad forms of patriarchal repression with absurdist, ironic and satirical humor—inviting the reader to conspire in ridiculing some of the most painful issues of our times.

In his writings on the sublime, Peter Cochran reverts to Longinus' quotation of Sappho's Ode to show that the sublime does indeed unite, or in some manner bind together, opposites. Discussed earlier in with reference to al-Sa'dāwī's writing, it is worth repeating a few of Longinus' observations about the Ode he attributes to Sappho's in the context of al-Sammān's work:

> Is it not wonderful how at the same moment soul, body, ears, tongue, eyes, colour, all fail her, and are lost to her as completely as if they were not her own? Observe too how her sensations contradict one another—she freezes, she burns, she raves, she reasons, and all at the same instant. (23)

The conflicting extremes of passion, thought, being and becoming are plainly included in the sublime, but what of irony and ironic laughter? Peter Cochran explores Byron's defense of the sublime in *Don Juan* and concludes that his lordship has a more accurate grasp of the principles articulated by Longinus than his critics. In fact, in his letter of defense, Byron employs, "a number of techniques which

Longinus describes as ways of achieving a sublime effect" (226). That Byron, who studied the classics as a matter of course, could reproduce technical virtuosity is not in itself a compelling argument that his writing did, in fact, achieve sublimity. However, Byron convincingly contends that the sublime and bathos can co-exist, or what Byron calls "the quick succession of fun and gravity" (Cochran 120). The almost instantaneous contrast of the crudely embodied against the spiritual and refined may create bewilderment and disorder that approaches the sublime and is capable of producing a new world view. Cochran cites Longinus in this respect: "by the very audacity and recklessness of his inversions, he administers a much more powerful shock" (132). *Don Juan's* contrasts are often of a Falstaffian nature; the sublime and ridiculous are bedfellows. Such irony exposes the tripartite relationship between author, reader and story and strengthens the bond between author and reader. The author invites the reader to act in collusion to ridicule grim realities. Although she shares his irreverent earthiness at times, al-Sammān uses the sharpness of irony in a way that considerably differs from that of Byron. She sharpens the contrast of delicate psychological portraiture against boldly overdrawn characters, and the juxtaposition of humor against deadly serious matters, to administer shock. In al-Sammān's case, the picture is one of overwhelmingly pervasive corruption, widespread human destruction and misery for the sake of profit, and men and women both being trapped in the web of patriarchal power. D. C. Muecke argues that irony engenders a sense of detachment from the subject of the irony, and that, "this ironic spectacle has …an aesthetic quality which, so to speak, objectifies it" (64). Whether it is called perspective, or distance, or disconnection from the object, such a space between observer and observed is vital to the deconstruction of power imbalances. The detachment produced by irony is a feature of absurdist philosophy, which is threaded throughout *Night of the First Billion*.

The second comparison of the coexistence of irony and the sublime is found in *Invitation to a Beheading*. That black comedy is laced with terror and tragedy, but the sudden realization that the structures of oppression and enforced uniformity depend upon one's belief in them (which may be seen as the moment of ironic laughter) is the undoing of the entire construction; it crumbles and disappears. The irony combines with fear, dread, and metaphysical elements, to create a very distinctive type of sublimity. Although the comparison is made only to demonstrate that the use of irony can be both subversive and sublime, *Night of the First Billion* and *Invitation to a Beheading* have more in common that might be supposed at first glance. They both use humor (however dark) to demoralize the privileging of what John McGowan calls, "the concept of the same" and suppression of "differences in favor of similarities" (89-90). In both works, it is dangerous to be different. In *Invitation to a Beheading,* the play between reality and dreams contrast against the banality of tyranny (even when we have no clear idea of what is objective reality and what is not). The metaphysical "Otherworld" created by Nabokov extends into the realm of aesthetics and ethics (Vladimir Alexandrov 93); the world created by al-Sammān plays with different realities and delusions in an effort to escape the loss and devastation of war, quite differently extending into the realms of aesthetics and ethics through satire and irony. In both works, irony and fantasy are used together as tools of political, social and subjective revolution.

It is sedition with a difference, however, because there is no clear revolutionary message. Irony is essentially ambivalent and therefore, non-polemical, non-didactic and the very opposite of the dictatorial mandate. Walker contends that, in using irony and fantasy, "authors must maneuver around the language of dominant discourse in order to deconstruct cultural mythologies, including the myths that women construct about their own lives" (22). She also observes the importance of developing the subject self in women's novels: "Dissatisfaction with the self as constructed by others leads women to imagine alternative selves, a conceptualization that extends into fantasy in the form of dreams, memory, and even madness" (22). Thus, the imaginal realm is a locus of discovery rather than escape in the sublime encounter. Firdaus's deeply symbolic dreams and memories, Zahra's instability and madness and, in *Night of the First Billion*, the dream-like, mad and fantastical are different ways of dealing with the woman as being and woman as becoming. Walker goes on to explain that irony and fantasy are part of women's "resistance to the status quo of oppression" and that "fantasy—even when embodied in madness—explores alternative ways of being, while irony questions the fixity of conventional reality" (22). Both these tools are harnessed by al-Sammān in her Beirut trilogy, and particularly in *Night of the First Billion*.

## 4.1.3 Negating evils

Walker persuasively argues that irony is a linguistic device that, "forces a re-evaluation of the meaning of a text" (24). In order to suggest the density and complexity of lived experience, al-Sammān does not attempt to reproduce or duplicate "real life;" she creates instead a text that invites comparisons with genuine experience, consideration and re-evaluation. Walker also points out that irony is ungoverned by the "rules of right and wrong, truth and falsity" and that the collusion between author and reader created by irony "testifies to a shared consciousness of necessary though unsettling change in women's relation to cultural expectations" (23). Her definition of irony includes, "verbal irony, ironies of circumstance, and double narrative perspectives that challenge the immutability of perceived reality", all of which are deployed by al-Sammān in her resistance to the domination of cruelty, which inexorably victimizes women and men alike in *Night of the First Billion* (23). By employing instead an unexpected panoply of weapons, all of which rely on humor, al-Sammān is asking the reader to refuse and reject the evils she depicts. Some of the images and characters she conjures are exaggerated and cartoonish, but they are recognizably true within their falsity.

Al-Sammān's strange juxtaposition of the real and unreal, which ambiguates objectivity and subjectivity, is a fundamental part of her purpose. The interrogation of what we hold to be true is a basic function of feminist thought, especially those truths that are unquestionable. Thus, Walker presents irony as an important weapon in the feminist arsenal. Al-Sammān is exceptionally skilled in its deployment against patriarchal thought systems and women's complicity in reproducing and perpetuating the structures that oppress them.

## 4.2 Parody and satire in the feminist sublime

Amongst other methods, al-Sammān constructs counter-realities through the use of parody and satire. First, we will look at parody as counter-narrative that can speak truth to power indirectly, and second, address satire for feminist purposes. Ziva Ben-Porat defines parody as, "an alleged representation, usually comic, of a literary text or other artistic object – i.e. a representation of 'modeled reality,' which is itself already a particular representation of an original 'reality'" (9). Thus, parody requires a doubling, or even a trebling of realities. Rather like a woman looking at a painting which depicts her looking at a painting of herself looking at a painting, the parody mimics art more than life. Seymour Chatman believes that parody stems from the tension between "a known original" and "its parodic twin" (24). Double or twin messages in al-Sammān's work are embedded on many levels—in the narrative structure itself, in the diegetic voices, in the situations themselves—always undermining the constructions she is (re)presenting. Susan Fraiman has dubbed this "counternarrative." Tellingly, Linda Hutcheon reminds us that the Greek root of the word parody means "counter-song" (201). It has also come to refer to comedy with elements of the grotesque or ridicule, but these are not required. Expressing dissidence through parody has a long, vibrant literary history, which is beyond the focus of this chapter. In an interview with Alfred Appel, Jr, Nabokov defined the difference between satire and parody: "Satire is a lesson, parody is a game" (n.pag.). *Night of the First Billion* is both a lesson and a game, unafraid of the grotesque, fragmented identities, ambiguity, and irrationality. Hutcheon has defined parody in a feminist context: "Parody is one of the major forms of modern self-reflexivity; it is a form of inter-art discourse" (2). One of the purposes of this study is to encourage self-reflection in reading the three novels under discussion. In an interview with Kathleen O'Grady, Hutcheon notes that "parody is put to use by the marginalized women are often in the position of defining themselves AGAINST a dominant culture or discourse" (22).

The subversion of authority through parody is an ancient practice, perhaps as old as authority itself. However, one of the criticisms against both parody and satire is that the characters can become one-dimensional polemical puppet figures. As we will mention later, al-Sammān avoids this and other potential pitfalls, with the richness and multiplicity of the voices she employs. One of the purposes of satire is to cause reflection, re-thinking of accepted practices, and to effect social change. Is such an ambitious project realistic?

Speaking truth to power sometimes requires an indirect approach, and both parody and satire can play an important role in the literature of resistance. Where open criticism might be met with disapproval or even danger, parody or satire might get past the censors. However, numerous authors have commented on the general and somewhat surprising absence of women from the field of satire, suggesting that al-Sammān has shown extraordinary courage in occupying such a masculine space (Kunzel 3). Firstly, we will look briefly at definitions of satire and secondly, even more briefly, at women's use of satire in the quest for greater feminine subjectivity.

## 4.2.1 Satire

Ben-Porat defines satire as "a critical representation, always comic and often caricatural, of 'non-modeled reality,' i.e., of the real objects (their reality may be mythical or hypothetical) which the receiver reconstructs as the referents of the message. The satirized original 'reality' may include mores, attitudes, types, social structures, prejudices, and the like" (9). By focusing on realistic issues and mocking them, satire acquires a moral stance. Ben-Porat's definition accords with both Nabokov's "lesson" and Hutcheon's emphasis on the social and moral aspect of satire. Robert Elliott noted the unconciliatory and sometimes vituperative nature of satire. "All satire attacks something" (22). In remarking on the antagonistic and destructive nature of satire, Christine Kunzel cites Brummack's definition of satire: "aesthetically socialized aggression" (2). By extension, *Night of the First Billion* could be considered a sublimation of the calamitous social-economic, moral and political impulses al-Sammān satirizes.

Kunzel believes that the fact that aggression is taboo for women may undermine their participation in satire. Its use to achieve a feminist sublime seems even more unusual. "The prohibition of female aggressiveness, and even denying its existence, has a long tradition" (3). She cites Musfeld in remarking that, even today, this is something of a blind-spot in feminist interrogations of constructions of femininity (Musfeld 17; Kunzel 3). Susan Purdie notes that those who make jokes can establish themselves as masters of discourse, and thereby seize ideological power: "And in patriarchy, the power of joking significantly supports and is appropriated by 'natural' male authority." (147)

Satire, then, has the potential to hijack ideological power, and destabilize social and moral constructs. No wonder it seems widely to be considered a masculine preserve. Al-Sammān's novel is just such an "assault on an outrageous reality" as

Kunzel suggests comprises satire (3). The novel is both intellectually and emotionally engaging on many levels, and while the satire is acidic, it is not savage. Zita Dresner states that, "Perhaps because women have had a history of coping with powerlessness, lowering their sights, modifying their needs, and compromising their desires, their humor has been less volatile and nihilistic than men's" (153).

We find such skillful, biting, revelatory satire in the works of women writers from early modern through modern times (Margaret Cavendish, Jane Collier, Maria Edgeworth, Jane Austen, Edith Wharton, Margaret Atwood, Fay Weldon and many others), that it may be possible to overlook the relative dearth of women writers employing satire. Yet its potential to transform can be both revolutionary and sublime, and its relevance to the exploration and rewriting of feminine identities seems important. Bakhtin reminds us of laughter's anarchic, destructive quality— especially its ability to destroy fear (23).

Common criticisms of satire include that distance is imposed between observer and observed, and characters are reduced to the level of caricatures, resulting in a lack of empathy for them, and that it presents a one-sided moral, social or political perspective. While all of these points may be valid, it seems that al-Sammān moves beyond such limitations. The distance between the reader and the characters in *Night of the First Billion* allows the reader to perceive them more clearly, and does not seem to be an estrangement. On the contrary, even the repellent characters are also imbued with some attractiveness, complexity and interest. The entanglement, fragmentation and multiplicity of voices (even within a single character) prevent the oversimplification of unilateral representation.

Purdie posits that the language of jokes and poetry is similar, in that both involve "unusual attention to signifiers" and "excess signification" (8). There is a poetic and dreamlike quality to *Night of the First Billion* which sits strangely with its caustic sarcasm, and merciless exposure of the immensely profitable masculine war machine, and its unwitting network of socio-cultural and political supporters. The juxtaposition of corporate revenues with human torment is an inherently aggressive aesthetic.

Purdie goes so far as to propose that jokers can "break and keep the basic law of language, and consequently in controlling possession of full human subjectivity" (5). If al-Sammān's novel contains lessons, aesthetically socialized aggression, and mockery, they are turned on the socio-political, cultural, class and economic constraints to the attainment of full subjectivity, and the processes by which we re-enact and re-enforce limitations on ourselves and others, and stay trapped in pain. As we will discuss in the following sections dealing with the main characters she satirizes, al-Sammān's use of wit as a weapon to deconstruct unacceptable realities is ultimately a positive form of aggression because it is transformative.

## 4.3 The uncanny in the sublime – Raghid

In *Night of the First Billion*, even though Kafa is the predominant female protagonist, she is surrounded by important figures, which makes her story seem less important in a sense. Her life story is one of many who have been displaced by the war. *Night of the First Billion* does exactly not revolve around Kafa, although her transformation is the focus of this study. Al-Sammān uses the classical structure of symmetry for her interwoven stories. Each character has a shadow or double, as one commonly finds in ancient Roman literature and the European literature inspired by it, particularly in the 16$^{th}$ through 18$^{th}$ centuries (*The Menaechmi* by Plautus of ancient Rome and Shakespeare's *Comedy of Errors* being perhaps the most obvious examples). This classical architecture is not employed by al-Shaykh in *The Story of Zahra* or al-Saʿdāwī in *Woman at Point Zero*—the authors employ non-linear, fragmented narratives. In the case of *The Story of Zahra* where there may be a sort of doubling (for example, between the stories told by Zahra, her uncle and her husband) but the effect is entirely different than the doubling used by al-Sammān. Symmetry, along with al-Sammān's deft use of irony and magical realism, are amongst the points that set her writing apart, so we will pay some attention to characters other than Kafa. The villain, the magician and Kafa's double (her husband), are archetypes that all deserve some consideration. They affect her life and play a role in the transitions she undergoes from living in Beirut and losing her daughter, to the disintegration of her marriage, the move to Switzerland and her final social death as she embraces prostitution. Raghid, one of the characters Kafa meets in Geneva is an outrageous parody, yet al-Sammān's portrayal is nonetheless chilling because it is recognizable.

Like al-Sammān's other works, *Night of the First Billion* is imbued with elements of Arabic folklore, tradition and myth. Terror and the mysterious properly belong in the realm of the sublime. Clearly, not all frightening incidents must entail an encounter with the sublime, but the potential for sublimity through fear has been mentioned earlier, and is exploited by al-Sammān at times in this novel through characterization and the wartime circumstances.

Al-Sammān has created a frightening antagonist, Raghid Bey Zahran. A war profiteer who collects women and gold, he can be absurdly reminiscent of an egomaniacal villain of the type found in the James Bond novels of Ian Fleming. While irony is a recognized tool of absurdist literature, this uncanny or disquieting weirdness is an unusual feature. Al-Sammān permeates her tale with the uncanny, especially through Raghid and his pet magician, Shaykh Watfan. Raghid is an inversion of what it means to be human—a double, or reversal of humanity. "Everyone detests me, even my guard dogs. Returning hatred for hatred, they loathe me secretly while I loathe them to their faces. Could love take any other form?" (al-Sammān 25). But in an odd twist, al-Sammān also uses irony and satire to destabilize the very structure she creates. Not entirely unlike the character, Auric Goldfinger in

Ian Fleming's James Bond novel, *Goldfinger*, Raghid's only loves are gold and power; he is manipulative, sadistic, and without a trace of compunction. By turns terrifying and ludicrous, he is always calculatingly and deliberately evil. By making Raghid cognizant of his own evil, al-Sammān has added a curious dimension of self-awareness to a tale that combines horror, the uncanny, and the metaphysical. It may also be suggested that this element is what distinguishes al-Sammān's portrait of Raghid from more nuanced depictions of psychopathic criminals. It causes him to resemble a cartoon villain. "I take unabashed pleasure in hatred, and I glory in performing its base, despicable rights" (25). Unapologetically evil, he cites his wealth as the reason he can indulge in immorality without check or hindrance. A cynical reader may see the truth of this at once. Raghid is symbolic, in that he represents the dehumanization caused by war. The darkly absurdist aspect of his character is nihilist in that is serves to highlight the futility of the patriarchal social, political, and economic systems that dominate our world, despite all reason and rationality to the contrary. Numerous critics have remarked that amongst all the devastation al-Sammān's work sounds a hopeful note. This researcher suggests that this is precisely because she rejects hope. One of the paradoxes of absurdism is that in repudiating hope, one may find freedom. From the absurdist point of view, hope is a fraud. Al-Sammān is extraordinary in that she mixes the uncanny with absurdism as a form of creative rationalism; she simultaneously rejects and exalts the irrationality of existence. In so doing, she invites the reader to engage with existential questions and challenge their own preconceptions.

Raghid is suggestive of Arabic tales of ghouls that drive people insane, kill, and crave and thrive on dead bodies. Jilali El Koudia and Roger Allen set out Moroccan folk tales in which ghouls appear; in one story, featuring a girl brought on misfortunes, including a ghoul who ultimately kills her years after she killed him, because of her greed (1-6). The *Unheimliche*, or uncanny, weaves a spell of unnerving fear and fascination, which can instantly border on the sublime. As we shall discuss in detail, al-Sammān uses mythic folkloric elements and fantasy to destabilize the sense of an incontrovertibly objective reality. Adrian Johnson suggests that Lacan's foremost contribution to modern thought is his insistence that "[N]on-existent, fantasmic elements play a necessary, constitutive role in the forging and sustenance of human experiential reality, and that these (unconscious) fantasies, although variable, resist unrestricted modification at the behest of the subjected subject" (429).

In *Night of the First Billion*, the real and unreal are woven together to create a new, indefinite, chaotic fabric of reality.

## 4.3.1 The ghoul

As with irony, the use of mythology or folklore and the uncanny to undermine generally accepted reality intimately and immediately involves al-Sammān's reader in the continued creation of the text. Hélène Cixous writes "between the text and its reading, in this enticing interplay where the text always emerges a step ahead, the doubtful elements of the text necessarily engender in its reader" (526).

Al-Sammān is well-known for her use of the owl and other images that reach deep into some Arabic cultures. The ghoul has been widespread in Arabic folklore since pre-Islamic times. Ghoul mythology evidently originated in Mesopotamia. Not implausibly, Ahmed al-Rāwī suggests that Bedouins were in close contact with the nearby sedentary civilizations for the purposes of trade. *Gallu* was an Akkadian demon of the underworld "responsible for the abduction of the vegetation-god Damuzi (Tammuz) to the realm of death" (Lindemans n.pag.). Since Akkad and Sumer were very close to the Arabian deserts, Arab Bedouins in contact with Mesopotamian cultures could have borrowed the belief in the ghoul from the Akkadians" (2). Although their conclusions are contested, Peter Holt and Ann Katherine contend that the advent of Islam failed to change some fundamental and prevalent aspects of pre-Islamic "Arab culture," such as pilgrimage to Mecca and belief in supernatural beings, djinn and ghouls. Hence, in their view, such rituals and beliefs were integrated into popular, and sometimes canonical, Islamic practice (17).

According to Ahmed al-Rāwī, Abī al-Shaykh al-Iṣbahânī (c.887 - c.979), al-Qazwīnī (c.1208 - 1283) and Hasan el-Shamy in his catalogue of folktales, accounts vary considerably: the ghoul may be a female demon, a shape-shifter; it may have a semi-human or animal form; it may have magical powers; it may possess human bodies, and is associated with madness and deformity in humans. Ibn Durayd (C.E. 838-933) calls the male ghoul "Quṭrub" (1121) and *mârid* ("rebel" which also means gnome, goblin, imp, or little devil in English) is a well-known demon which may also be identified with the ghoul (al-Zubaydi 165). The ghoul makes frequent appearances in Arabic literature ancient and modern, from the famous tale of the second rightly-guided Caliph 'Umar (c.586—644 CE) killing a ghoul in the desert to modern novels.

Al- Rāwī highlights some ghastly stories from the C.E. 14th and 17th centuries as well as el-Shamy's classification of the, "Ghoul (ogre) as hybrid of *jinniyyah* and hyena" (104) as evidence for the ghoul that, "digs graves and eats corpses in Arabic sources" (4). This hyena-like ghoul can bewitch people. "It has the ability to change its form and become a beautiful woman to attract men or even to mate with them. The ghoul's description is close to that of a predatory animal that has fangs and cloven feet, and combines features of the snake, goat, and ass" (5). In *Night of the First Billion*, Raghid is predatory and monstrous, and metaphorically devours the dead; the sale of arms is his chief source of income. He requires the services of a magician to bewitch people, but he uses devious forms of deception in the mundane world to ensure that the war is profitably prolonged, including carefully planted explosives to trigger greater violence, co-opting politicians and corrupting the voices of poets and popular figures.

> I never married and I never had children so that I wouldn't have to pretend to love them. However, I regret that. I wish now that I'd had children, children I could have hated and been hated by in return without the slightest embarrassment. After all, as a well-to-do man, I can afford to be a beast…. (al-Sammān 25)

Hasan el-Shamy, in his encyclopedic work on Arabic folklore, suggests that one's "life space" holds a fusion of the real and the imaginary worlds (7). Al-Sammān's use of fantasy and folkloric elements goes even further to suggest that the reality of the imaginal world is no less real than what may be generally regarded as objective reality. The interrogation of subject/object, and the dichotomies of reality and being, are at the heart of the feminist sublime, which may ask more questions than it provides answers. Al-Sammān use of figural devices, such as ghoul and owl, which are laden with meanings in Arabic consciousness in ways that simultaneously suggest reality and unreality accomplishes just that.

Al- Rāwī cites Gerda Sengers' study of "popular Islam," referring to localized, non-canonical religious practices, which mentions the exorcist ritual called "zar," involving the recitation of verses from the Holy Qur'ān (23-4). Ironically, the magician employed by Raghid exhorts supernatural beings to do his bidding, but Raghid himself is not subject to exorcism. He continues to commit heinous acts until he is murdered.

Raghid dedicates his entire existence to hatred and destruction. He floats in his pure gold swimming pool, a womb in which he experiences a parody of the masculine sublime. In his hierarchical, transcendent sublime, he is exalted and reigns supreme, but instead of achieving understanding and tolerance his sublimity is inverted and merely exaggerates his contempt for others.

> Here was no longer any time, or space, or history. Rather, he himself was time. He was space. He was eternity. … Here, he could go beyond everything to its true, inner reality: the all-encompassing grandeur of the cosmos that surpasses all of people's trivial concerns … In this prayer niche of his, he could glorify the one thing that truly possessed him and held power over his being: hatred. It was a pure, unmitigated hatred …. (37)[13]

---

[13] In the original Arabic, this is Pp. 36-37:

هنا لم يعد له زمان ولا مكان ولا تاريخ... انه الزمن والمكان والأبدية. لم يعد الابن الشاطر للتاجر الميسور سامي الزهران المهدد بالافلاس رعبا من قوانين التأميم وعبد الناصر, لولا تولي الابن مقاليد الأمور في الوقت المناسب... هنا يتجاوز كل شئ إلى حقيقته: العظمة الكلية المتجاوزة لتفاهات البشر كلهم من حب وألم ومرض وموت... وفي محرابه هذا يمجد الشئ الوحيد الذي يقطنه ويستولي عليه: الكراهية. الكراهية المقطرة للآخرين .

-"the clever son" الابن الشاطر
(In the original text, الشاطر) is embodied with negative characteristics that describe an evil-minded malignant, fiendish, nefarious, sneaky and vulpine person. This description becomes crystal clear with the wicked methods that Raghid used to collect his fortune. He did not help with his father's bankruptcy by being "clever"; rather he helped him by being "sneaky".

In that environment, Raghid becomes free from concerns about his physical appearance and limitations and free from fear. In a further perverse twist on transcendent oneness, he becomes one with gold, the element that "had been manipulating the destinies of men since the beginning of time" (37). His "sublime" is an extreme of the masculinist sublime, in which transcendence is marked by the subjugation of the other and aggrandizement of self.

Raghid is the double or reverse of life's ontopoiesis, a distorted being given to the overt and covert annihilation of others. In a sense, he is also Khalil's opposite or double: Khalil has dedicated himself to ideals in direct resistance to Raghid's, and Khalil is protected by a supernatural force against the attempts of Raghid and his tame sorcerer to exterminate him.

In his work on the experimental Arabic novel, Stefan G. Meyer, commenting on the earlier volume in al-Sammān's Beirut trilogy, states that her, "most important innovation in *Beirut Nightmares* is the interweaving of chronological narrative, fable, and dreamlike situations. In some of the narrative sections…there is a clear symbolism. …the animals have an obvious reference to the human inhabitants.…" (159). He distinguishes three types of narrative in that work: the experiential; the creative; and the reflective (122). "Experiential" refers to the day-to-day experiences of the hero, which are set out chronologically. "Creative" refers to the stories inserted into the narrative: "By producing such stories, the narrator is able to delve more deeply into the war…" (124). "Reflective" refers to dreams and imaginings that are part of the narrator's experience, "yet more than this; they are reflective of a greater horror than can be summed up by a mere recounting of daily events that occur in her personal life" (125). *Night of the First Billion* also contains innovative narrative, which in different ways makes the widespread and far-reaching horrors of war almost tangible. Much of the book is set in Geneva, rather than Beirut; what the war loses in immediacy, it gains in size and scope. It is a vast octopus, whose tentacles strangle its victims from a distance of thousands of miles. It corrupts and destroys men and women across continents. As with *Beirut Nightmares*, in *Night of the First Billion*, animistic, folkloric and uncanny elements are employed to appeal to primeval modes of thought in a clash with the severe rationalism which marks absurdist literature. The conflict between the natural and the supernatural, real and surreal, can act both in opposition and in concert to establish a space for the sublime.

Al- Rāwī asserts that the belief in ghouls (and the djinn and demons of various sorts with which ghouls are sometimes conflated) is prevalent today. The iniquitous Raghid is obsessed by magic and attempts to control destiny and others through the supernatural. Figuratively, he possesses the bodies of others, causing people to do his will by cunning, deception or force, no matter how repugnant to them it is, and ceaselessly manipulating them not only for his own benefit but also for the sheer malicious pleasure of causing harm. His association with madness and deformity is undeniable—he distorts, corrupts or destroys everyone within his sphere of influence. His inhumanity is complete, but his likeness to a ghoul or other imaginary and unsavory creature does not obscure the fact that his acts are all too regrettably human—particularly war profiteering. In his portrait, al-Sammān offers truth within the caricature.

## 4.3.2 Absurdity, monstrosity and the uncanny

Through this absurd character, al-Sammān reminds us that war is big business, with tentacles stretching from Beirut to Geneva and beyond. Raghid's obsession is carried to bizarre lengths—he has a gold staircase leading to his pure gold pool, which his surrounded by a gold carpet, gold-plated chairs with gold-thread embroidered cushions, and gold statues representing the major world currencies on gold plinths (36). However, in the absurd we find liberation; Albert Camus famously asserted that the absurd is the essential concept and the first truth (17). Raghid may be a caricature and quite unreal, yet he is an all too recognizably factual a part of the modern economy, which requires fresh blood to feed the military-industrial institutions. Raghid's political adroitness and complicity in prolonging the war may remind readers of the situation in which many now find themselves where developed countries have enormous and highly specialized arms industries that depend on conflict to survive. These industries are distributed throughout small and large cities and provide vital jobs. On Jan. 17, 1961, President Eisenhower warned the American public famously about the grave implications of a large arms industry—a development unprecedented in history. In previous wars, existing industries converted to the manufacture of weapons and then, after the war, reverted to making instruments useful in peacetime. Advanced technologies meant that it was no longer possible for Ford Motor Company, for example, to make arms and then revert to manufacturing automobiles. Eisenhower cautioned that the, "very structure of our society" is involved in the newly specialized arms industry, and that, "[t]he total influence—economic, political, even spiritual—is felt in every city, every State house, every office of the Federal government" (n. pag.). Raghid grossly emphasizes the profound moral dilemmas created by a new economic system, which must have war. It may be suggested that many economies of the past required military conquest and colonialism to exist, such as those based in Persepolis, Athens, and Rome, and that Raghid may represent an eternal type. But it may also be that he represents a uniquely modern, perhaps Nietzschean type, devoted solely to destruction. Specialization is a modern phenomenon. Modern specialization has led to the development of men who are dedicated purely to damage and devastation, to whom the threat of peace is the threat of extinction.

Such men are monsters. Al-Rāwī says that in traditional Arabic literature, men and women were often compared to ghouls, sometimes indicating merely ugliness or forcefulness, but often to emphasize an evil characteristic (8). Animal and ghoul allusions respecting Raghid are not explicitly articulated and are merely suggested, but Raghid *is* horrifying. "He would have loved to be able to kill off the entire population of Planet Earth at the moment of his own demise" (al-Sammān 26)[14]. His inhumanity is so complete that he resembles some unreal being, yet even without any such association, his unswerving commitment to destroying people is uncanny. While this study is not based primarily on psychoanalytic principles, nonetheless Freud's uncanny and Cixous's feminist reading of Freud's uncanny are not out of place here. It may be argued that the uncanny can play a crucial role in the sublime. Freud suggests that the uncanny represents different things to different people. The words he contrasts are *Heimliche* and *Unheimliche*, meaning literally "homely" and "unhomely" (unfamiliar), respectively. The English word has analogous meanings. As Cixous notes, "canny" can mean either "cosy" or "endowed with occult powers" (643). In his famous paper on the subject, Freud comments that very little literature is to be found, "upon this subject in comprehensive treatises on aesthetics, which in general prefer to concern themselves with what is beautiful, attractive and sublime—that is, with feelings of a positive nature—and with the circumstances and the objects that call them forth, rather than with the opposite feelings of repulsion and distress" (525). Al-Saʿdāwī creates the uncanny and the sublime through the radical defamiliarization of everyday scenes and situations that Firdaus undergoes. Al-Shaykh explores the uncanny through Zahra's psychological disintegration; the ordinary became extraordinary, disturbing and strange. Al-Sammān reaches the uncanny through her use of animal allusions (octopus, owl, bee, and beast), Raghid's horrifying deeds, and the magician's conjurations. She also employs the surreal, as in the circus scenes, with vivid, unnerving effect. Khalil is taken to a bizarre, nightmarish circus while he was under the influence of hallucinogenic drugs. He witnesses what seem to be insane shows that are deeply disquieting mockeries of real life. In the circus, women refuse to do any work outside the home, men refuse to try to better their condition because only what is written will come to pass, and once revolutionaries win their battle, they become the new oppressors. Pauline Homsi Vinson highlights the similarities between the parodies and reality. "It is easy to see how the different episodes in the circus represent the sad state of Arab, and especially Lebanese, life as Samman sees it" (n. pag.).

---

[14] In the original Arabic, this is p. 27   إنه يشتهي ان يقتل سكان الكرة الارضية كلها لحظة موته
-He would have loved to إنه يشتهي
(in the original text it is "desire/crave"; he "craved" to kill). "He would have loved to" implies a state of weakness, as he loves to do something but he might not be able to do it; while desire is a strong drive that reflects his inner craving for blood. He is hungry "to kill off the entire population of Planet Earth". For example: there is a huge difference between a person who loves to eat an apple and a hungry person who craves to eat an apple. The first might not mind not finding an apple to eat and might settle for another option as a replacement for the apple that he could not get. But the person who craves an apple desires nothing but having his apple and this becomes a strong drive for him to get to his goal; he won't settle for the idea of replacing it with something else.

## 4.3.3 Uncertainty and the uncanny

Al-Sammān achieves that mysterious "Disquieting Strangeness" that Cixous elucidates. Further, Cixous speaks of the mixture of disgust and attraction, repulsion and pleasure in the uncanny, in a similar language used by Burke when he describes the vacillation between attraction and disgust in the aesthetic sublime. The precise nature of the relationship between the sublime and the uncanny, however, is elusive.

Hélène Cixous comments on Freud's unsettling ambivalence regarding the *Unheimliche* "As a commentary on uncertainty…nothing turns out less reassuring for the reader than this niggling, cautious, yet wily and interminable pursuit (of 'something'—be it a domain, and emotional movement, a concept, impossible to determine yet variable in its form, intensity, quality, and content) (525).

This "something" is akin to the negative emotions that can feature prominently in the sublime, such as torment and terror. It is difficult to define, yet the indefinable may well belong to the sublime—the shifting world of transition, in which one does not yet know where or who one is or who one will be, for example. The vague stirrings of revulsion and attraction to a character such as Raghid, subconsciously evokes the sublime. Cixous argues that "The indefiniteness is part and parcel of the 'concept' (528).

Indeterminacy can be part of a process—although one does not know where it will lead or if it will, in fact, lead anywhere new. A state of being which is caught in a question, or an almost-question, in which one has not yet articulated the question, has been described by Lyotard as a "sublime event" (event being defined, at least in part, as a lingering but unknown question. He describes the sublime event as a recognition of potential, "the feeling that something will happen, despite everything, within this threatening void, that something will take 'place' and announce that everything is not over" in *The Inhuman (84)*. When we stop questioning the sublime event, "we shut down its capacity for transformation," however, indefiniteness allows us to "maintain the specificity of the event and respond with openness to the challenge of its radical indeterminacy" (Shaw 122)). Freud encourages indefiniteness and questions everything, but in the end, one is left with the impression that what comprises the uncanny for one person may not be so for another. What should and should not be revealed is surely a matter for personal ethics and morality, socio-cultural influences, and reflection, as Cixous writes, "*Unheimliche* is the name for everything that ought to have remained… hidden and secret and has become visible" (529). It is what should have remained hidden, and thus, we step into the realm of repressions. She also highlights the incompatibility of the uncanny and irony, which, arguably, al-Sammān has transcended in *Night of the First Billion*. Further, al-Sammān navigates the contours of war and sexuality in a manner that is utterly unlike that of al-Shaykh, however, as miriam cooke highlights, this is an important topic not only for both of these authors, but also other women authors of the Lebanese war. The fantastical yet strangely authentic Raghid sits at the intersection of the real and the imaginary, in an attempt at redefining subjectivity not only for women but also for men, as a critically important, fundamental move forward in the deconstruction of patriarchal oppression.

## 4.3.4 The uncanny and the magician

Like Prospero, the sorcerer Shaykh Watfan in *Night of the First Billion* lives in a world of his own, in which the usual rules pertaining to life do not seem to apply, at least temporarily. The magician's incantations are eerily evocative and suggestive of worlds beyond our understanding and control. However, the reader may understand such episodes to belong to the safe realm of the imagination, in which the usual laws of physics are suspended, and there is no conflict of judgment. The lack of ambiguity and wonder therefore softens or even eliminates the uncanniness of his acts. In fiction, much of what ought to be uncanny is not, yet there are far more opportunities to create the radically and disturbingly unfamiliar with fiction than with non-fiction. Cixous comments on this paradox: "a great deal that is not uncanny in fiction would be so if it happened in real life" (639).

The magician, a figure worthy of fairy tales, Tarot cards and the like, ought to elicit feelings of dread and the uncanny, but it is questionable as to whether he succeeds. Cixous points out that that fairy tales, some of the stories from the Old Testament and the like, in which the dead are revived and other incidents bordering on horror are described, tend to be an exception. They fail to evoke disturbing sensations.

The difference is that in most respects, *Night of the First Billion* is realistic; hence, the possibility for creating radical defamiliarization exists despite the overtly fantastic elements. Associated more with South American than with Arabic literature, magical realism is a remarkable tool against colonial and patriarchal oppression because it appeals directly to what Henry Corbin argues is our stagnating, trivialized, and degraded imagination. Corbin deplored the superficiality of supposing the imagination is mere fantasy, rather than an important intellectual faculty. To Corbin, the neglect of the imaginal realm is tantamount to the failure to cultivate the intellect. The imagination is the mediator between the real and non-real, the realized and the immanent, the known and the unknown. Al-Sammān entreats the participation of and nurtures the reader's imaginative faculties, which in turn opens the space of the sublime with all of its possibilities for transforming being into becoming.

Speaking of *Beirut Nightmares*, Meyer writes, "[S]ometimes there is no clear dividing line between dreams and imaginings and the diary narrative" (127). Similarly in *Night of the first Billion*, al-Sammān blurs the borders between the real and the non-real (or surreal or hyper-real) in order to create sublimity. By deliberately confusing being and non-being, and fact with fantasy, she renders our conception of reality suspect. As we noted in the previous chapter, al-Shaykh calls into question what we perceive as reality in *The Story of Zahra*, with disturbing and sublime effect. Al-Sammān confounds the mythological and nightmarish with the commonplace forces reflection and re-conception, interrogating the nature of reality itself, in her highly textured, ambiguous and disquieting narratives that seem to suggest biocentric scientific hypotheses, such as those espoused by Dr Robert Lanza who asserts that humans continually project the internal onto the external, that is, that the universe does not exist in a state independent from the observer. Dr. Lanza states that, "…while we are in the process of sorting out the fact that time and space don't exist without us, our reality will feel like a bit of madness" (2). Al-Sammān embraces the temporary madness of the sublime through the magician.

Like Prospero, perhaps dramatic literature's best known magician, al-Sammān's magician lives in seclusion, but he is not on an uninhabited island that he can control. The spirits, demons, djinn and supernatural beings that the sorcerer conjures up assuage his personal pain, as he slides deeper and deeper into the occult, and eventually into madness. He has made a Faustian pact to relieve himself of unbearable pain and poverty, but cannot enjoy the harvest of his dark labors. Unlike Prospero, he knows that he is actively, deliberately harming people who themselves have done no harm. Also unlike Prospero, he is serving a monstrous, ghoulish master for pecuniary gain. Therefore, when he encounters the one man he cannot injure—Kafa's double, Khalil—the magician is deeply threatened. The connections and reciprocity between reality and unreality in the scenes involving the magician produce the potential for the uncanny, as well as the sublime. The reader's suspension of disbelief in *Night of the First Billion* is not total, as in a fairy tale in which the rules of engagement are already understood. The book opens with a scene that could have been lifted out of a summer blockbuster action film, yet nothing about it is inherently unreal. It is dramatic and thrilling, but perfectly believable. Similarly, nothing about the magician is unreal, except perhaps only the practice of magic, and the widespread belief in his practice engenders a different response than would a fairy tale. Thus, the sorcerer creates ambivalence about our assumptions regarding objective reality and how we ourselves and others construct our reality. This can be also take the form of what Cixous calls "reality testing," in which the appeal to our more primal, animistic beliefs may be answered by already-existing rational thought, or in the alternative, stimulated by al-Sammān's narrative and subjected to newly-imposed rationality.

> Let us take the uncanny associated with…secret injurious powers…. We—or our primitive forefathers—once believed that these possibilities were realities, and were convinced that they actually happened. Nowadays we no longer believe in them, we have surmounted these modes of thought; but we do not feel quite sure of our new beliefs, and the old ones still exist within us ready to seize upon any confirmation. (Freud 247–248)

This masterfully describes the process similar to that which al-Sammān employs to stir deeply held, unexamined beliefs through the imaginal realm and the uncanny.

## 4.4 Kafa's transitions

The female sexed body, such a profound and pivotal element in *Woman at Point Zero* and *The Story of Zahra*, is not neglected in *Night of the First Billion*. The female body is a war ground. It is also a source of meaning. Kafa is the only hero of the three to have children. Her maternity and the loss of one of her children is a complex field of abjection, pain, and fear of further loss. She remains a highly sexual being despite motherhood, an aspect of her being which is rigorously repressed and ignored. In her discussion of Bracha Ettinger's and Julia Kristeva's conceptions of the maternal sublime, Griselda Pollock highlights the multiplicity of the maternal-feminine, which, "could be understood as a thinking apparatus for human subjectivity that goes way beyond the utilitarian process of generating little humans. It is a matrix for other logics, for ethics, for aesthetics, for poetics, and even for social relations perhaps" (13). Al-Sammān's symmetrical multiplicity in *Night of the First Billion* treats the maternal sublime on numerous levels, exploring its hidden imaginal, intellectual and emotional potential, through Kafa's transitions and metamorphosis, and arguably, through the transitions of her shadow or other self, Khalil.

In speaking of feminine subjectivity, Pollock necessarily speaks of the female body as well, setting forth the feminist parameters of the Arabic women's writing examined herein, which is distinctly feminist not because of its subject matter but because of the manner in which it addresses subjectivity (12). The distinctive ways that al-Saʻdāwī, al-Shaykh and al-Sammān engage with binaries such as subject/object, real/unreal, and other social, political, cultural and personal constructions is feminist in a far deeper sense than that their writing is about women and their bodies, women's experiences, and their resistance to patriarchal domination. The exploratory, experimental, developing subjectivity of women seeking the fullest possible experience and expression of their being is embedded in the writings investigated in this paper. Refusing and even ridiculing the restrictions of misogynistic thought, these writers enable liberational reflection through the interaction between text and reader. Pollock suggests that what we need to do now is, "think about subjectivity as a plaiting of the Real (the traumatic), the Imaginary (the realm of fantasy and images) and the Symbolic (words and thought), a weaving of the corpo-Real, the fantasised and the signified" (12). The works of al-Saʻdāwī, al-Shaykh and al-Sammān interweave just such elements and answer this need.

### 4.4.1 Escape from war

Both al-Shaykh and al-Sammān address women in the Lebanese war. In *Night of the First Billion*, however, the protagonist Kafa manages to escape Beirut to Switzerland with her husband and two surviving children, after seven long years of planning. Thus, for the first time in her Beirut trilogy, al-Sammān allows the reader to understand some of the far-reaching ramifications of war. Her merciless pen lampoons everyone from the politicians who sit in the pockets of billionaires, to the idealistic and truth-loving fools who are prepared to sacrifice everything for their dreams of a better Lebanon. There is a surreal and cinematic feeling to the narrative, as al-Sammān shifts viewpoint, tone, scene and reality, and flits from character to character in a complex web of money, power, sex and war.

We are introduced to Kafa after a portentous opening in which the magician performs a solemn incantation. It is followed by a dizzying, dangerous escape from enemies on the way to the airport, as the family is leaving for Geneva amidst simultaneous air raids and ground attacks. Al-Sammān immediately reveals her mastery of multiple narratives and reality-challenging shifts; she uses magical realism to present the paradox of the simultaneous contrast and togetherness of opposites. Not only does al-Sammān depict Kafa's personal descent into hell and the transitions she undergoes, but she also depicts that of Lebanon as a whole. As soon as Kafa is more or less safe on the plane bearing her, her husband Khalil and her sons to Switzerland, al-Sammān grants the reader insight into the broken relationship between Kafa and Khalil, and the similarly maimed relationship between truth and politics, idealism and war, which grips Lebanon. Kafa thinks:

> While my sisters were living in the lap of luxury with their husbands in this country or that, I was stuck in a city polluted with bomb blasts and violence, haunted by the ghost of hunger, and filled with worry, disappointment, shattered glass, the scattered remains of loved ones' mangled, decaying corpses, and caravans of suffering humanity. (17)[15]

The repeated loss of her husband as he is imprisoned "without even knowing exactly why or where or who's against whom" has shattered her belief in the power and efficacy of truth. The sacrifices she has made for his sake and for the sake of their country are neither recognized nor valued. The historically almost complete exclusion of women through war is finally broken by the women writers of the Lebanese conflict, who are at last able to make their voices heard over the screaming of rockets. Kafa finds her own way out of war, but Geneva doesn't give her the freedom she expected.

---

[15] In the original Arabic, this is p.18

بينما ترتع شقيقاتي مع ازواجهن بالبحبوحة والامان في اقطار العالم الراقية.. وانا ساقطة في مدينة موسخة بالانفجارات. العنف. شبح الفقر، قوافل البؤساء. القلق. خيبات الامل. الزجاج المحطم. الاحباب المتناثرة اشلاؤهم.

-"I was stuck in" وانا ساقطة

In the original text Kafa describes her status as a "fallen woman" in this chaotic city; where being a female has its hidden cultural implication that reflects her to-become status of a "fallen woman" though she continues respecting her social bonds as a daughter, a wife and a mother. Once she arrives to Switzerland; she chooses to become this "fallen woman" that she never was while living in Lebanon. "I was stuck" reflects a physical status of not being able to move out or in; "I was a fallen woman" has a strong indication of her cultural death without even having sinned yet; she is dead by just having being born in her female body.

-"caravans of suffering humanity" قوافل البؤساء

In the original text it is "caravans of les miserables" which has a strong indication of the cultural injustice that Victor Hugo described in his famous novel *Les Misérables*. However, in France it was only les miserables, while in Lebanon it is caravans of les miserables.

The disillusionment with "truth" ultimately drives Kafa to make her own truth. It has also driven a wedge between her and what may be regarded as her other self, her shadow, her counterpart—Khalil. Both the fragmentation of her being and the gulf between the idealistic dreams for Lebanon and the gruesome reality are underscored by the breaking of the once ardent bond between them.

> Oh, I was so passionately in love with the fool, and now I don't know anything anymore. Once upon a time I fell madly in love with him because ... he never said anything but the truth just the way his villager father had taught him. Little did I know that the very thing that I loved about him would become the thing that makes me miserable with him! All the catastrophes that have hit us have been on account of telling the 'truth'—or at least what he imagines to be the truth—wherever he happened to be and whatever the circumstances, demanding 'the right to dialogue'! The idiot. (17)[16]

In this case, al-Sammān lets Kafa's voice be heard. When we examine her husband's view of the same events later in this chapter, we discover that Khalil is also aware of his foolishness in thinking he could make a difference in the outcome of the war through his integrity. The role of the fool in telling the truth to power is explored by Lacan, an aspect that will be discussed when we address the character of Khalil in greater detail.

The narrative voice then changes to third person, which provides distance and adds irony even while describing a painful situation. Both first and third person voices make it clear that Kafa demeaned herself for love and truth. She married into a lower social stratum, and the sacrifices which that entails are no longer justified. She no longer believes in truth as a force for good, or more specifically, what Lacan refers to as the "Sovereign Good." Khalil, who may be considered her shadow or other self, has valued truth more than personal relationships, and more than the safety of his person. A man of unbending principles and a rigorous sense of honor, he is an extreme of an admirable type. Carrying such admirable qualities to an extreme is, in Kafa's view, impractical and dangerous. They are estranged, but still closely connected.

---

[16] Unfortunately, at this point the translation lets the reader down. In the original, this is Pp. 18-19:

آه ذلك الاحمق الذي كنت اعشق، والآن لم اعد اعرف شيئا.. احببته بجنون ذات يوم لانه رائع لا يقول الا الصدق، كما علمه والده القروي. ولم اكن ادري ان مبرر حبي له سيتحول يوما الى مبرر بؤسي معه!.. والمصائب كلها التي تعرضت لها واسرتي، كانت نتيجة مباشرة لاصرار هذا الاحمق على قول الصدق او ما يتوهمه صدقا اينما كان كيفما كان... مطالبا ب"حريته في الحوار"! الاحمق!

- "have hit us" تعرضت لها واسرتي
In the original text it is have hit "me and my family". She does not consider Khalil and herself as "us"; she has not melded into his ways of thinking or living. Here we have two different states of being. One reflects unity "us" while the other reflects division "me and my family"; Khalil is the cause of her miseries; he is not part of her life. The subjective "I" is strong in "me" and "my family" that reflects her individual personality; while "us" does not reflect her state of individuality.

- "have been on account" نتيجة مباشرة
In the original text it is "a direct result of". This reflects her state of anger and frustration on the one hand because his insistence on telling the truth is the only cause for all "the catastrophes" that have hit her and her family; it is not simply "on account" it is rather "a direct result".

- "have been on account of telling the 'truth'" كانت نتيجة مباشرة لاصرار هذا الاحمق على قول الصدق
In the original text she is angry while in the translated text Kafa sounds calm. Also in the translated text the word "fool" has been omitted and the word "insistence" which both reflect how angry she is.

Cixous describes the self's double as the "ghostly figure of nonfulfillment and repression, and not the double as counterpart or reflection, but rather the doll that is neither dead nor alive" (540). If Khalil is the embodiment of Kafa's nonfulfillment, she is his lost sensuality. Khalil's devotion to truth sublimated his passion for his wife; their relationship is no longer physical, but he is not unaware of her power to enchant and bewitch men. On the airplane to Geneva, he pretends to sleep in order to disguise his torment over what's going on around him. The sight of Nadim in the first-class compartment, a wealthy Lebanese man who, "lives in all the capitals of Europe at one time" stimulates Kafa's "forgotten passion for gold doorknobs, private airplanes, marble-floored living rooms and fur coats, diamond earrings, credit cards, caviar, crepes suzette, and lobster" (18). Her electrifying effect on Nadim is palpable. The narrative voice shifts abruptly to Kafa's other self, as Khalil realizes that the journey will be an eternity of humiliation for him: "It's as though from the very first step I took out of Beirut, I set my feet down in the wrong place, keeping company with the very people that I'd once almost paid with my life for taking a stand against" (20). He loathes the man to whom his wife is casting lures, "[t]he self-exiled rising star who would sell anything: arms, women, nations, airplanes, petrol….", yet Khalil is rapidly heading towards a place where people like Nadim reign supreme and will be able to exercise a more subtle but nonetheless comprehensive power over his life (19). In Beirut, Khalil was strong, active, and capable. When they have been out of Beirut for a period of mere hours, the transfer of power, activity, and strength becomes apparent. Khalil and Kafa have separated and become opposites. As Kafa ascends, Khalil sinks. They cannot rise together.

## 4.4.2 In search of identity

In Beirut, Kafa was not wanted by her parents because of her gender. Once she defies her family by marrying beneath her, she is forced to accept Khalil's destiny as her own (93). She goes directly from a family and a society in which she has been othered and inferior because of her sex, straight into a familial situation in which she is the shadow or adjunct of her husband. She does not have an identity of her own—she is defined by what she is not, and in relation to another ("the daughter of…", "the wife of…"). As Khalil's sexuality is attenuated or sidelined by his commitment to fighting ideological battles, a process which results in subsuming himself in the greater good and, to some extent, the loss of his individual identity in the group, so Kafa's sexuality is thwarted. As a woman, her self-expression, self-realization and subjectivity hinge upon Khalil. Luce Irigaray maintains that, in language, women do not occupy the subject position and do not express themselves as subjects as men do—linguistically, subjectively, conceptually, the construction of women's identities is at least partially dependent upon men and male values. This lack of an independently realized self haunts Kafa, and drives her to take strong action towards becomingness as a woman. Griselda Pollock reminds us that "The 'feminine' is always described in terms of deficiency or atrophy, as the other side of the sex that alone holds a monopoly on value: the male sex (18).

Kafa has an imperative to define herself as something other than a lack or deficiency. The instant Kafa steps out from under Khalil's dominance, she begins to send out siren calls, and flirt—if only with her eyes—with a man she finds attractive. An almost-forgotten identity and sexuality, long obscured, begins to burgeon even as she is on the plane to the land she has been dreaming of and scheming to attain.

Kafa's metamorphosis begins as soon as she is liberated from Beirut, a freedom she has achieved only by determination and sacrifice. "She spent everything she owned, including hers and her family's valuables, to bring him and her children out of danger" (57)[17]. Her primary concern is for the safety of her children after the death of her daughter: "The day Widad died, she felt she'd died herself. And perhaps she had" (199). Kafa desperately needs to experience fully and deal with her mourning, refashion her identity, and cultivate her own independent beingness. In their emotionally shattering showdown, Kafa and Khalil reveal the lack of a real relationship as husband and wife. Khalil's intellectual energy substitutes for or sublimates his libido; perhaps childishly, she blames Khalil for their daughter's death. She turns to materialism for easy comfort, perhaps the sole comfort she can find. Characteristically, we learn of the devastating scene between Kafa and Khalil only as a nightmare that Kafa revisits (96).

Khalil's political arguments and insistence upon the right to dialogue are sterile to Kafa after she has lost Widad. She tells him:

> What a brilliant theorist you are. You're so dazzled by your eloquence and your ability to lay out the facts just the way you'd like them to be, you don't even stop to notice Widad's dead body—Widad, our little girl. I avoid even mentioning her so as to spare both your feelings and mine. (94)

They each feel misunderstood and unrecognized. Khalil also complains that she doesn't notice who he really is (94). But Kafa is angry, full of blame, and disillusionment. "Five-year old Widad paid the price. Her death didn't serve the cause of liberating either Palestine or Lebanon" (95). Kafa signifies "enough" in Arabic, and she has had enough. She rebels against the authority automatically conferred on Khalil due to his masculinity

---

[17] In the original Arabic, this is p. 53:
لقد انفقت كل ما تملك من حلي الاسرة ومجوهراتها لتنجو به وبأسرتها.
-"to bring" لتنجو
In the original text it is "to save" ... "out of danger" and not just "to bring". She is saving her children from all kind of bad endings; for example, from dying, from being foolish and from going to war.
-"and her children" وبأسرتها
In the original text is " and her family". Saving his family is Khalil's cultural responsibility as a man to protect and save but here Kafa is the one who is taking the role of the savior; she is not only a mother who saves her children but she is saving her larger family unit. Also she uses her family's valuables (her parental family) to save her own family.

and insists that they leave Beirut. "Well, it's no sin to defend what children I have left. This city is no longer fit for children, or for ideas, or for fighting, for that matter" (96). She is haunted by the death of their daughter and regards the city as a graveyard. "Now that you and your buddies have taken over my children's play-grounds and left mines among their toys, I'm not going to let you kill any more of them" (96)[18]. The bitterness and rage she directs towards Khalil are, in part, due to unresolved issues of mourning her daughter and logically have little to do with him personally, but she has no space in which to be herself, to understand her loss and to come to terms with it. As long as she lives in a graveyard that threatens to consume the bones of her whole family, she will be relentlessly miserable. With some justification, Khalil accuses her of manipulating him. "You're just using her memory as a way to carry out your plans" (97). Indeed, she has been planning to leave Beirut for seven years, since the war started in 1975, so she has seized upon Widad's death to orchestrate their departure. But her stance, too, is justified and neither can truly empathize with the other. Later, reflecting on the profound changes in Kafa—her assertiveness, ability to take action, and even her longing for physical comforts as a substitute for her losses, the narrator says, "she'd changed a lot. The woman he married hadn't been like this" (152).

In war, encounters with death and near-death become daily occurrences. Though this daily violence ceases with their move to Geneva, both Kafa and Khalil undergo sublime events unlike anything they have experienced before. Kafa is confronted by the urgency of developing her subjectivity and an array of unpalatable choices. She is in some respects already dead, due to the loss of Widad, so it is not such a great step to progress to the complete social death that prostitution entails. Unable to move beyond anger and blame towards Khalil, "[h]e'd already deprived her of Widad, and her broken heart couldn't be broken again" (347-348).

## 4.4.3 The human situation as a whole

Al-Sammān seems to present Kafa's predicament as a microcosm and a social artifact. In *The Meaning of Psychology for Modern Man,* Jung asserts that, "every individual problem is somehow connected with the problem of the age, so that practically every subjective difficulty has to be viewed from the standpoint of the human situation as a whole" (429). Thus, without social proselytizing, the bitter choices that face Kafa reach beyond her to other women in wartime. Jung's research into both the personal and social function and nature of dreams is relevant not only to

---

[18] In the original Arabic, this is p. 86:
لن اسمح لك ولأصحابك بقتل المزيد من اطفالي بعد احتلال ملاعبهم وتخليف الالغام بين دماهم
-"have taken over" احتلال
In the original text it is "occupied" which has historical and political reflections of the Israeli occupation and the war in Lebanon. For Kafa, Khalil and his "buddies" who are occupying her "children's play-grounds" are not any better than the Israeli occupation which is partly what they are fighting against.
-"I'm not going to let you" لن اسمح لك
In the original text it is a strong voice say "I will not permit you".

Kafa, but also to most of al-Sammān's writings. Mixing dreams/nightmares and mythological images, al-Sammān contrasts the private traumas and transitions Kafa undergoes with the same in the public sphere, for Lebanon and perhaps even the Middle East as a whole. Joseph Campbell, speaking with Bill Moyers, spoke of the difference between dreams and myths, both of which figure prominently in al-Sammān's writing, "…a dream is a personal experience of that deep, dark ground that is the support of our conscious lives, and a myth is the society's dream. The myth is the public dream and the dream is the private myth" (n. pag.).

Campbell speaks of the outcast as being socially dead, but such a "death" can be part of one's quest: "If your private myth, your dream, happens to coincide with that of the society, you are in good accord with your group. If it isn't, you've got an adventure in the dark forest ahead of you" (n. pag.). Kafa's dream is not in harmony with her society's mores and she must suffer a social death in her pursuit of being and subjectivity as a woman. How to define and understand self, her womanhood and death is one of Kafa's key challenges; she must somehow live with the loss of her daughter. Like her daughter, Kafa undergoes death, only in Kafa's case, it is volitional—she embraces her own death as necessary. In order to understand death, one must form some idea of what it is that ceases at the point of cessation of life, whether it is social, spiritual or biological life. Jonathon Brown uses the term "extended self" to include those things that one considers one's own (my body, my chair, my pet, my family), which go beyond the common conception of self and yet are closely associated with who we are. Such places, people, and things are part of the psychological construction of self. Brown also cites William James, who, divided the *ME* into three subcategories: the material self (our bodies and extended selves), the social self (the various roles we play in social life and the way we are recognized and regarded by others), and the spiritual self (our inner or psychological self, including our ideas about our traits and abilities, values and habits, and the way it feels to be us) (46-47).

Understanding self in its broadest meaning is part of Kafa's quest. Like Firdaus in *Woman at Point Zero* and Zahra in *The Story of Zahra*, Kafa is on her own when she decides "enough!" and is compelled to seek meaning in selfhood and death. She has no guidance, no previous cultivation of the intellect to rely upon and assist her in her journey. The broad societal neglect of women's subjectivity has resulted in the women in the novels examined in this study being forced to negotiate being and becoming entirely on their own.

## 4.4.4 Social death

Michael Mulkay writes of social death as a process which may be of long or short duration, which may occur independently of biological death, and which involves treating the being as a "non-person" as defined by Mulkay: "that the actor has ceased to exist as an active agent in the ongoing social world of some other party" (60-61). In many respects, Kafa (like Firdaus and Zahra) has been treated as a non-person all her life: defined by lack; by inferiority; and by difference, they are not perceived as fully-fledged human beings. Kafa's choice to accept social death is thus emancipatory.

Kafa chooses social death as a means of attaining complete selfhood and autonomy, but it means losing her existing extended self—her family, her husband, her possessions, her identity. Her desire for Self, for genuine subjectivity, is not something she can articulate. She overtly desires the beautiful material things that give her comfort, almost in caricature of greedy, selfish Lebanese women. But Kafa does not merely desire luxury; she is driven by grief, loss and perhaps the most fundamental loss or absence of all, the lack of self.

Lacan's conception of the sublime object and ethics is relevant to the feminist sublime, and in particular to Kafa's experience. She accepts loss of identity and symbolic death in what she perceives to be a principled, moral manner—despite the fact that her actions are well outside the normative, particularly for a woman of her class. While this may be al-Sammān's oblique comment on the commoditization of women (much as Firdaus returned to prostitution after discovering it was not much different and far more honest than working in an office), it also hints at moral and ethical dilemmas and Lacan's interpretation of the tragedy of Antigone in the sublime. In a substantive sense, both Firdaus and Kafa transgress the social order and endure a form of death in order to be true to their desire and sense of ethics. To condemn them as immoral is to miss the point of the sublime altogether. Of course, it is understood that they have boldly stepped beyond societal boundaries. It should also be understood that their intent was strictly moral, in the same way that Antigone knowingly defies Creon's laws because she believed that they were wrong and contrary to authentic morality.[19] Kafa, believing herself to have been pushed to "point zero" begins to understand some part, at least, of the infinite potential of zero and deliberately defies her group's mores in order to experience her latent being. She has consciously chosen death; that it is social rather than biological death does not make it any less real or less final.

### 4.4.5 Some ethical questions in sublimity

The classical story of Antigone, interpreted by Jacques Lacan and Judith Butler, amongst others, provides some illustration of Kafa's pure ethics even in her immorality, and the sublimity of her social death. Lacan applauds Antigone's self-

---

[19] Antigone is the daughter of the unfortunate Oedipus and Jocasta. In the play by Sophocles, Antigone tries to obtain a proper burial for one of her brothers, which was forbidden by her uncle King Creon because he deemed that her brother was a traitor. Her defiance of masculine authority ends in tragedy for herself and those who love her, such as Creon's son and wife. Her name has numerous interpretations: *anti* (against) and *gone* (generative) suggesting anti-motherhood or anti-masculinity.

sacrifice as sublimely beautiful. Her decision to defy Creon "consciously seeks death" (323-325). Paul Allen Miller summarizes Lacan's interpretation of Antigone:

> Her choice takes her beyond the realm of rational discourse and the collective norms of human satisfaction it implies. ... Hers is a position that transcends the comfortable binary oppositions that structure our daily ethical and social lives. Because her choice of death cannot be understood according to strictly rational norms, she cannot be read as representing some simple antithesis of freedom to tyranny, or the individual to the state. (1)

Kafa, like Firdaus, Zahra, and Antigone, has gone beyond considerations of utility, beyond "conformity to a reality principle" in the practice of her moral doctrines, beyond preconceived limits, and she moves forward with an "ethics of creation as opposed to conformity" (2). She can no longer afford to be comfortable in the existing structure, and must rupture social norms in order to achieve a fuller, more complete Being or selfhood. Miller cites Irigaray regarding what may be interpreted as the crux of the feminine sublime experienced by Kafa, "There is an asocial immediacy to absolute enjoyment, to pure desire, which while profoundly ethical—in the sense of representing an absolute dedication to the transformation of self, which the realization of a desire beyond the pleasure and reality principles requires—nonetheless also figures a rupture with the Symbolic order as we know it" (14).

Kafa's commitment to her own metamorphosis takes priority over mundane considerations, and gives her an entirely new view of the social restrictions that have so successfully constrained her being and expression all her life.

But Antigone's beautiful sacrifice should not serve as a pattern or example. Unlike Sartre in *Essays in Existentialism*, Lacan tries to evade symbolic death or suicide. Lacan posits an in-between or middle ground in which one may avoid symbolic death and yet be true to one's desire, in a field that is essentially beyond commonplace assignments of right/wrong and good/evil while still remaining within the symbolic order (152). This may be problematic and does not seem to have been a possibility open to Firdaus, Zahra or Kafa. Žižek's view of the sublime differs from that of Lacan, but he too suggests a solution in, "the good that lies outside of what one can manage within the cracks of the symbolic order" (23). The feminist sublime is open but not limited to such a solution. Its exploration of and inclusion of the marginal, unrecognized and unrepresentable renders it appropriate to the discovery of hybrid solutions, that preserve some elements of the social order while allowing the subject to be true to herself. However, it may be that in some circumstances, this is impossible to achieve and only a complete transformation or transcendence will serve the ontopoiesis of life.

Paul Allen Miller posits an ethical dilemma that pertains to Kafa, as well as to Firdaus and Zahra, in their urge towards being through the feminist sublime, "...Antigone's refusal to recognize the claims of the law, her pure desire to transgress... leads her from the Symbolic death affirmed by the pleasure principle to the second death, which is its beyond. Her destruction is not the product of an error in judgment... but of a fundamental and uncompromising disposition toward Being" (11).

Al-Sammān creates tragic figures, but unlike Sophocles, she imbues their stories with irony and satire. Hence, characters such as Kafa are ambivalent and the reader must constantly question preconceptions and fixed moral, social, cultural, economic and political beliefs. Miller continues his interpretation of Antigone: "In her insistence on her desire to the point of death, a desire that transcends all rational calculations of Symbolically determined utility, ... she becomes both more and less than human, immortalized as a sublime figure of beauty in death, a figure of folly and awe. In the process, she becomes a profoundly ethical figure in her uncompromising singularity" (11).

Kafa, like Firdaus and Zahra, may be seen as a sublimely tragic and beautiful figure. In the alternative, Kafa may be taken as a superficial, empty-headed, pleasure-loving woman whose hunger for luxury and personal gratification outweighs all other considerations. On the contrary, she may be perceived as a distraught, grieving mother who has lost what mattered most, and casts off the rest of her old skin in a brave and deeply ethical compulsion towards Being. It may be that al-Sammān's greatest achievement is creating ambivalence and having the courage to leave questions instead of answers for her readers.

### 4.4.6 The surreal and the sublime'

The interplay of fantasy weaving in and out of Kafa's experiences and parenthetical thoughts lends her story a surreal quality. Al-Sammān has exaggerated Kafa's qualities and brought them out almost immediately upon introducing Kafa, such as her unsatisfied sensuality, her class-consciousness, and her lust for material things. Even though Kafa may be considered a parody of "typical" Lebanese women in European capitals—shallow, selfish, and motivated by money, she still has depths to reveal. Al-Sammān infuses her cartoon characters with such life that the reader may feel she or he recognizes them. Amidst the fantastical elements, Kafa and indeed most of the characters in the novel have distinctly recognizable personalities and histories. Al-Sammān's literature of desire emphasizes the stultifying effect of patriarchal socio-economic and political systems, whether in the midst of war or luxury, *Night of the First Billion* spares no one and nothing. Satire, magical realism, and poignancy combine to strike at the foundations of assumptions and highlight the absurd futility of war more efficacy than pure tragedy could achieve. Nancy Walker disagrees with theories regarding literary fantasy that: "emphasize its negation of actuality and possibility" and cites Rosemary Jackson, who has proposed that fantasy is heavily dependent upon a social context" (26-27).

Women and children—the silent and invisible in war and in peace alike—are brought forth to be heard and seen in Arabic women's writing. Al-Sammān's imposition of fantasy and folklore on the strict rationality of absurdism mocks patriarchal authority, negating it in ways that intellectual or passionate arguments cannot. Her dramatic imagery and rapid shifts of scene lend al-Sammān's writing a cinematic quality. A similar sort of wicked, wry and painful comedy permeates *Night of the First Billion* as *Dr. Strangelove or: How I Learned to Stop Worrying and Love the Bomb*—a thorough and unabashed political satire that can change the reader's views and attitudes with appeals to reason and emotion through mockery. Kafa's transitions, as microcosmic travesty of that of many Lebanese women, have a special social relevance, demonstrating the recreation and reenactment in exile of the social and economic dynamics that contribute to and perpetuate the war.

Fantasy, the uncanny, irony, primitive and animistic components, such as magic and animal images, combine to weave a complex tapestry of which Kafa's transitions are only one portion. However, her role reversal, strength and dedication to transformation through acts of pure ethics, give her evolution compelling importance in the picture of women's and men's liminality, being and becoming in wartime that al-Sammān has given us.

## 4.4.7 Kafa's maternal sublime

The maternal sublime has been discussed previously, and is mentioned briefly here in relation to Kafa. Griselda Pollock, in her evaluation of Ettinger and Kristeva's apprehension of the maternal sublime, points out (in accord with Kristeva) that we are "the first civilisation to lack a discourse on the complexity and meaning of motherhood" (17). The conflicted and abject domain of maternity and motherhood as Kafa experiences it is the field of personal subjugation, objectification, and pain. Her identity is constructed around and is dependent upon her husband and children. The abrupt loss of her only daughter—a relationship that is absolutely unique in her life—sends her spiraling into a grief from which she cannot emerge. For Kristeva, this unique relationship is a complex generative source of abjection and repression, anxiety and what she terms maternal passion. "For Kristeva, such passion is pregnant with both madness and sublimity" (Pollock 17). Resisting the "denial of maternal passion seen in the media and in the biological and social treatment of motherhood", Kristeva calls attention to the importance of maternal function in the development of subjectivity. Further, she rejects theories posed by Freud and Lacan in which the child enters social life under the aegis of the paternal function, as she sees the maternal as prefiguring Paternal Law. Thus, in a logic that goes beyond the norm (phallo-centrism), the maternal is fundamental to the human subconscious. Kristeva suggests that we are always "subjects-in-process" and holds the maternal body forth as a pattern for all subjective relations—we are always negotiating the Other within. The "two-in-one or other within" is embodied by the physiological maternal, but psychologically it is the always part of the process of being.

In *Mothers and Daughters*, Marianne Hirsh cites research by Chodorow, Flax, and Dinnerstein that suggests that girls' different subjective development may have meant that Kafa and her daughter were attached to one another as one being, undifferentiated and connected (207). Thus, Kafa really did die when Widad was killed. "Feminine personality comes to be based … more on retention and continuity of external relationships… The basic feminine sense of self is connected to the world, the basic masculine sense of self is separate" (Hirsh 213). Hirsh further cites Signe Hammer's study on mother/daughter relationships to highlight the subtle differences in the interactions between mothers and their daughters, including the fact that a young daughter does not see her mother as a separate person (213). Because she identified with Widad on a very basic level, Kafa's trauma is intensified.

The abjection of the maternal helps to illuminate the contours of women's oppression in patriarchal cultures in which women been reduced to reproductive function. Kristeva believes that the answer lies not in refusing motherhood but in opening a new discourse on a subject which has long been dictated by masculine institutions: church (motherhood as sacred) and science (motherhood as biological). The feminist sublime offers ways to gain experiential, intuitive and intellectual knowledge respecting motherhood. The maternal sublime offers a language that can validate the experiences of the subaltern, the in-between and marginalized, who are normally excluded from representation. The processes of the maternal sublime as proposed by Freeman and Yaeger are marked by inclusivity, connection, and expanding, spreading rather than elevated awareness. The maternal sublime is a special experience capable of shedding light on the operations of oppression and belongs in the feminist sublime.

### 4.4.8 Kafa's other self

Kafa was once intensely in love with Khalil and his truthfulness. As she becomes increasingly disenchanted with the high cost of telling the truth, she also becomes jaundiced about Khalil's truth—she understands that his truth is relative and personal rather than an overarching truth for all of Lebanon. He is her opposite in many respects. They are reverse mirror images of each other. Where she is demanding, physical, and fiery, he is intellectual and cool. She embodies the chaotic, generative female force, while he embodies the epistemology of masculinity: rationality. As usual with al-Sammān, things are not quite as they seem. When they leave Lebanon, their roles are reversed. But Kafa becomes masculinized only so she can realize her femininity in a fuller sense. In Geneva, Khalil is more trapped by class barriers than he was in Beirut; he becomes feminized, passive, and feels like a prostitute. The downward trend already noticeable at the airport, where he looks like Kafa's servant, worsens; he becomes demoralized while Kafa starts to blossom. But what a blossoming. Al-Sammān gives Kafa a cynic's awakening, as Kafa, already far more materialistic than her idealistic counterpart, soon makes herself into a commodity for men. Kafa and Khalil are at polar opposites, and in their respective sublime encounters, they fail to find a way forward together.

Natural beauty, the locus of the Romantic sublime, is the site of a different sort of experience for Khalil. As he gazes at Lac Leman, wondering at the people who could see such beauty "without feeling guilty, terrified, or confused" he undergoes a crisis of emotion and identity (97). The elements of the classical sublime are present, from breathtaking natural beauty to terror and other strong emotions, but Khalil does not become exalted. Unlike Raghid's parody of the masculine sublime, in which his uplifting experience magnifies and pays homage to hatred, Khalil sinks deeper into a grief so acute that it is physical. Where Raghid is ironically ennobled by overpowering, all-consuming hatred, Khalil is rendered tragically vulnerable. His sublime encounter with overwhelming stimuli is essentially feminist, in that it acts as an intensifier.

> He was overcome by an extraordinary sense of grief, a feeling akin to nausea in the face of a beauty so resplendent that it can neither be touched nor contained, ... The sight reminded him of Kafa's body, the thought of which made him feel ashamed and humiliated. After all, she'd been turning into the man of the house—taking the children to school and spending her own money on them while he lay sleeping in a posh hotel the likes of which he couldn't afford for even a single night. He felt about as respectable as a hooker who doesn't get up till noon. (97)

Because he and Kafa are adversarial, the reversal of roles in which Kafa is now dominant, means that he must be subjugated. The ideologies to which he has devoted himself and his family—whether they wished it or not—betray him. The sublime's potential for non-adversarial resolution, or union of opposites, is not exploited. His daughter is dead, and he is homeless in a strange land. His wife blames him for Wadid's death, but he no longer really blames her. He is haunted by the emptiness of his political convictions and the sacrifices he made—and required his family to make—for those beliefs. Khalil's sad memories of Wadid are more painful for his own failure and the failure of a political movement which degenerated into promiscuous murder. "She'd been playing to the rhythm of gunfire that was directed at the enemy only once for every thousand times it was directed at friends" (110).

Kafa is chiefly concerned with herself, and ostensibly with her family. Khalil is her socio-political opposite, but his courageous embrace of sacrifice—and death, if necessary—in his choice towards pure ethics has gone awry. "He'd longed to give Widad a homeland fit to grow up in. But instead she'd been blown up by a shell bearing the words, 'For freedom and democracy'—words his beloved comrades had forgotten in the heat of their fruitless warring" (110). He does not feel the bitterness towards Kafa that she feels for him. "He looked affectionately over at Kafa. He blamed her and didn't blame her. Or rather, he didn't know anymore whether he did or not" (110). She offers to treat him to coffee or Coca-Cola, further underscoring the role reversal and her dominance, his relative uselessness. The Coca-Cola in particular triggers memories for him, as a ubiquitous symbol of the Western imperialism and capitalism that threatens his country—and here he is, in Geneva, actually drinking the beverage prohibited by political awareness and the convictions of his comrades. Like Kafa, he faces unpalatable choices. He feels it is inhumane to deprive their little boys of their homeland; it is inhumane to expose them to the dangers of their homeland (111). Al-Sammān invokes carnival, masked men, dreams and nightmares in Khalil's sublime, which is distinctly feminist in nature. He is consumed by indeterminacy and ambivalence, and must find or fashion an identity for himself that he can live with. Like Kafa, this involves sacrifice and the relinquishment of long-held beliefs, and social death.

### 4.4.9 Ethics and the fool

Both Khalil and Kafa blame their troubles on Khalil's insistence on speaking the truth. Kafa labels him a fool for trying to have open dialogue with the kinds of maniacs who torture people. Traditionally, an "allowed fool" (in Shakespeare's phrase) was given great license to speak truth to authority without fear of reprisal. Lacan associates the character of the fool with left-wing activists, not unlike Khalil, giving him an ethical mandate to speak the truth *because he can* (182).

To Lacan, foolishness is linked to sovereignty and ethics. Much has been made of his arguments regarding sovereign good and sovereign unity. With respect to Khalil, the most important points are firstly, that he could not, in fact, speak the truth without fear of reprisal—he was constantly suffering arbitrary detention, imprisonment, and fear of torture and death—and secondly, the subversion of the sovereign good, in which the good becomes bad when it is forcefully applied to people collectively rather than individually. Khalil's reminiscences, in which he wonders how he and his comrades became so murderous over minor differences in the implementation of essentially the same ideology, make it clear that he stood in more danger from his friends than from his enemies. Khalil takes purely ethical acts in the Lacanian sense: he is acting neither from self-interest, nor pressure to conform. Žižek, commenting on Lacan's critique of Antigone and the sublime object, explains: "choice thus represents a pure ethical act shaped neither by a self-interested selection among communally recognized goods nor the self-loathing of conforming to a code that is recognized and despised" (77). Žižek is speaking of Antigone, but his conception of a purely ethical act applies both to Khalil and to Kafa; whose choices challenge conventional rationality and moral codes, yet are undertaken with highly principled intent. Khalil's failure to understand that the role his father gave him, that of an allowed fool, was no longer viable and placed his family and himself at grave risk. Because of Khalil's inability to understand his position in a changed world, Kafa was forced to dominate and "become the man" of the family, which in turn triggered further transitions for both of them. However, both Khalil and Kafa, as reverse images of one another, experience the feminist sublime. Lacan's notion of the development of subject as a consequence of processes is relevant to the sublime encounters here, because of his emphasis on ethics and his understanding of identity and symbolic death. The feminist sublime may be a single, shattering event, but it also may occur as a lengthy process. Both Khalil and Kafa do undergo dramatic and traumatic wartime encounters that may constitute the sublime. They also experience incidents that reinforce and maintain the processes of sublimity. Whether in Beirut or Geneva, the civil war continues.

## 4.5 Symmetry and sublimity

Double, non-linear and circular narratives are amongst the innovative features of Arabic women writers. Where al-Saʿdāwī repeatedly uses the circle in both symbology and narrative structure, and al-Shaykh utilizes fractured, interwoven narratives to reflect the fragmentation in awareness brought about by the war, al-Sammān uses doubling on different levels. Her characters suggest doubling, in the sense of being personifications of egos that are essentially complementary opposites. In *Night of the First Billion*, al-Sammān may hint at a fundamental philosophy: we are not complete without our opposite. She pits identity against alterity through the double, reflection, or shadow of each major character. Doubling is found in primitive animism (see Otto Rank, Freud, and Cixous), which al-Sammān stimulates by the use of folkloric, mythic, supernatural and animal images and figures. *Night of the First Billion* works on both psychological and non-psychological bases. In his psychoanalytic study of the double in literature, Robert Rogers notes, "the psychodynamic underpinnings of the story support and energize the non-psychological import, as may always be the case in fiction" (19). Perhaps it is not necessary to understand those underpinnings, but such an understanding must enhance one's own being. Finally, al-Sammān uses a subtle form of doubling—symmetry—in the structure of the narrative itself. In these ways, she opens the door to the unspoken inner world of her characters, inviting reflexivity, and both intuitive and rationalistic understanding.

In a manner which is both psychological and aesthetic, al-Sammān uses symmetry contrasted against asymmetry alternately to balance and unbalance. Psychologist I.C. McManus cites Dagobert Frey: "Symmetry signifies rest and binding, asymmetry motion and loosening, the one order and law, the other arbitrariness and accident, the one formal rigidity and constraint, the other life, play and freedom" (159). The banal arises in excessive symmetry and order; an excess of chaos is difficult to face. Al-Sammān exploits the tension between an essential harmony and the disorder that allows for growth. I.C. McManus reminds us that however appealing symmetry is, it can give a sense of fixity and stasis that is antithetical to life: "The ur-structure of much art, just as in biology, is symmetry, but some asymmetry is added to that symmetry to generate interest and excitement... Symmetry and asymmetry are therefore an essential dialectic for both science and aesthetics" (177).

Al-Sammān weaves a multiplicity of threads in both symmetrical order and asymmetrical anarchy in order to facilitate and highlight the feminist sublime, even while parodying or making light of it. She is unusual in achieving both irony and the sublime in the same breath.

I.C. McManus describes the urge to break strict symmetry in art, as well as "the social, biological and physical worlds, where despite an overwhelming desire on the part of scientists to find symmetries, the world does seem resolutely to be asymmetric at all levels, despite the best efforts to make it otherwise" (159). Al-Sammān's characters come together in symmetrical order and part in disorder, in an intricate and changing web of relationships and doubling. Kafa and Khalil are doubles. But Khalil and Raghid are also doubles. No, Raghid and Bahriya Zahran are doubles. Actually it is Shaykh Watfan and Bahriya who are doubles. Doubling and looping, al-Sammān's parenthetical narrative repeats and parallels, diverges and comes together again. *Night of the First Billion* has been compared to gothic romances, murder mysteries, and post-colonial magical realist novels. While it may incorporate features from all of these literary modes, it speaks with its own voice and creates a complex series of evolving relationships entirely its own. Al-Sa'dāwī and al-Shaykh use doubling in different ways from that of al-Sammān, but in all three cases the ultimate effect as it relates to the sublime is the same: it highlights non-linearity, and enables intuitive lines of thought and feeling that might not otherwise have occurred to the reader.

### 4.5.1 Dunya as two women

In a sense, Dunya is her own double. Parallel with Kafa's, Dunya's encounter with the sublime leads to dramatic changes. She looks at herself in the mirror and sees the contrast to the woman she used to be before she married Nadim captured in a painting, "How I hate this mirror and the picture of me hanging beside it, where I see two different women without knowing which of them is me. Who am I anymore, really? And what would I want to do if I were free again?" (48). Her lack of independently realized identity resembles Kafa's incompleteness, and for the same reason: she is married, and her husband takes first place in everything. Al-Sammān's subtly doubled or symmetrical narrative structure reflects sublimity in all the characters, even if the sublime is a travesty (as in the case of Raghid).

Dunya looks at the Self she used to be in the painting, and briefly becomes vibrant, recalling her drive to achieve her dreams and desire to be connected with others. "Why does my spirit burn with bitterness and disappointment whenever I shake off the numbing effect of this gilded crowd, whenever I'm alone with my sorrows and start thinking about this painting of mine?" (48). She feels an urge to accomplish something she has forgotten, to become herself, to complete herself. Dunya's self-image, what she sees in the mirror and what she sees in her painting are parodic representations of a fragmented Self. The disparate external images are at odds with her own image of herself, reflecting the disintegration of her Being. Which image is fake? Can they all be real? Or are they all self-constructed illusions? Trapped in an oppressive marriage, straight-jacketed by societal restrictions, Dunya's multiple, conflicting identities are mirrored still further by her husband's constant shift of identities.

Dunya muses on Nadim's succession of faces and asks the million-dollar question: who is he, really? Which of his many faces is really his, and why does he wear these masks? "Or is it that all these masks are actually a succession of incarnations of his one, true self, which has no independent existence apart from them?" (49). Dunya cannot answer the question about her husband or herself.

Dunya experiences a revelation and radical defamiliarization that almost reaches the sublime, but her courage fails. "The moment of awareness was so intense, it was like a lightning bolt that nearly split her head in two. It was as though she was seeing these people for the first time. As though she didn't know what she was doing here, and had just happened to fall into the house from some other planet" (51). Unlike Firdaus, Zahra and Kafa, she cannot let go of what she has become in order to become more fully herself.

Al-Sammān has been accused of indulging in didacticism in her Beirut trilogy. However, for the careful reader, she elicits more questions than she gives answers. The nature of being as a social construct, whether we do in fact have an independent "self," what it means to achieve subjectivity for women, and the feminist sublime are contested fields to which al-Sammān offers no simple answers. Like al-Saʿdāwī and al-Shaykh, she portrays the feminist sublime as a searching, expanding awareness rather a triumphal transcendence that preserves oppositional dualities. This experience is relative rather than absolute; it is liminal and in-between rather than decisive and final. It is not an end, but a progression in a process. Dunya must free herself from living in the shadow of a man and being his mere appendage before she can experience her own being and potentiality. This process is uncomfortable, and yet she must accept the implications of bewilderment as she negotiates being and non-being in order to become. In language that almost precisely duplicates Khalil's state, Dunya says, "I float, and I sink. I remember, and I forget. I vacillate in confusion, then I become sure once again that I detest him. ... there's no salvation for me unless he disappears, or dies" (49 and 97).

Al-Sammān employs a mirrored or parallel effect extensively but subtly. In Dunya's case, one may be reminded of the words of the protagonist in *Invitation to a Beheading* about doubles. He claims that we all have a double, who is "doing what we would like to do at that very moment, but cannot" (25). Mentally, perhaps we each have another Self who is breaking rules, ignoring conventions, and defying norms. In a sort of twofold symmetry, Dunya has a double within herself, and outside herself in the form of her husband.

## 4.6 The reader and sublime text

Ultimately, the author has no control over the text once it has left her pen. It now belongs to the reader, who fashions it in his or her own image, perhaps deriving meanings never intended by the author. Paul Allen Miller, in writing of Lacan's Antigone as an allegory of readers' encounters with a text, believes that, "the encounter with the sublime object is one that must shake us to our very core" and meeting our obligation to the sublime text means that we, "must go beyond the dictates of the pleasure and reality principles, beyond good and evil to encounter pure desire: the moment in which the canons of meaning shudder before their own beyond" (14). Achieving an understanding of Kafa's transitions may be regarded as acquiring a greater understanding of the nature of Self, collectively and personally. One of the objects of this study is to provide questions rather than answers, to encourage a reflexive reading of Arabic women's writing in the quest for fully realized women's subjectivity. A feminist sublime reading is necessarily inclusive of the marginal, in-between and inferior. It seeks understanding and coexistence rather than a reversal of the roles of domination. Thus, the reader may have an obligation not only to the text but also to herself or himself to be open to the encounter with the sublime in al-Sammān's writing.

# 5  DEATH AND CONTINUITY IN CONCLUSION

## 5.1  The sublime as a feminist framework

I have reviewed writing as diverse as parody, satire, and tragedy, the rewriting of patriarchal mythology and symbols in a feminist cast, magical realism, and folklore, employed in the search for identity and autonomy through the sublime. Notably, in utterly different ways, non-linearity and shifting views and voices were used to unsettle the narrative and problematize easy assumptions about both Zahra and Kafa. All three of the heroes demonstrated depths of strength through their pain that allow them to experience transitions in the sublime, and to embrace the end of one identity in order to become another—even where becoming themselves would result in physical or social death. Each of the novels deals with death in some manner. There are, of course, other interpretations of this thrust towards being or becoming, and death.

With regard to being-towards-death and what that death may actually mean, Elizabeth Langland speaks of death and paradigms in novels written by women about women: "Death or even suicide in novels by women writers is thus reinterpreted as a gesture of reaffirmation, a refusal to submit to society's dictates. Of course, we must always feel the poignant irony of a fate which demands self-destruction as a mode of self-assertion and self-definition" (87). The second pattern she describes in women's novels is the stunted personal development in the hero, and an awakening and growth toward autonomy, generally after adulthood and marriage. This may lead to adultery, disastrous consequences, or suicide, after the heroes are denied self-realization, self-expression, and self-determination.

Given that the three novels discussed herein generally fall into these broad patterns, is it necessary to propose another theory to analyze modern Arabic women's writing? First, in order to summarize the three "deaths" and the sublime experiences undergone by the three heroes, we would like to highlight the role of death in the ontopoiesis of feminine subjectivity. Secondly, from a feminist sublime view, we will underscore the positive aspect of the three deaths, while problematizing the potentially facile "economy of the redemptive" (to borrow Rosi Braidotti's phrase). Finally, I will briefly review why this researcher argues that there is value to a feminist sublime reading, and discuss how this study may accomplish its aim of deconstructing the mental mechanism of patriarchal oppression, that is, fixed dualities.

## 5.2 Death and continuity in the feminist sublime

Death is important to the stories reviewed in this study—the self-chosen death of Firdaus is probably a far stronger statement to society than anything else she could have said or done; Zahra's death, like her story, is ambiguous, and questions linger after her story is told; Kafa's death is social, and perhaps cynical, but complete. But why does death play such an inescapable role in the feminist sublime? We have seen multiple deaths in the stories reviewed—not only the physical deaths, but the deaths of identities that the heroes had adopted at times. Firdaus dies as a wife to become a prostitute, but she still does not find her true self. So she has died as a prostitute and became an office-worker. In a sense, Firdaus dies and is reborn numerous times before her execution. She has tried new identities, at first with the fresh new eyes of naïveté, later with clear-eyed cynicism, as in the second time she has become a prostitute in her quest for independence and freedom. In discussing the pivotal role of betrayal in Zahra's life, Semia Ḥarbāwī cites the feminist Jungian scholar Demaris Wehr:

> Women . . . need to 'die' to something before a new self can be born . . . Perhaps women . . . need to die to the false system that patriarchy has imposed on them, whatever form it has taken. This is not the same thing as the annihilation of the ego but dying to the false self would necessarily precede the birth of the true self (Demaris Wehr qtd. in Fido 336-37). (Harbawi 4)

This tends to explain the important part death plays in the sublime. Zahra goes through radical defamiliarization and rebirths, sometimes abortive, in her attempt to become a new person and to give her marriage another chance; at times it is also dramatic, as with her active role in seeking out and becoming the lover of the sniper. Kafa can no longer tolerate the person who she has become in Beirut, and eventually utterly repudiates all ties to the past when she turns her back on husband and sons. The birth of the true self cannot be achieved without a death of one kind or another, metaphorical or otherwise.

As we have seen, the masculine or feminist sublime experience is distinguished by whether or not it preserves or undermines the oppositional binaries that construct our conceptions of gender. The "quantum leap" in feminist thinking has been the discovery that dualities, fundamental to Western thought, play a role in the oppression of women. The sublime may provide another tool in the project of deconstructing the very foundation of the oppression of the "other."

The three novels analyzed in this study may appear superficially to reinforce the very binary oppositions that are used to build the machinery of oppression, whether institutional or individual. The heroes essentially kill themselves rather than submit to oppression. Socially, physically, or even metaphysically, they die. Is there really no escape from overwhelming and pervasive oppression other than death? Their lives and deaths may inspire a great deal of thought on the subject of Being, Being-toward-Death and Being-beyond-Death, which is the nature of the construction of self.

As noted above, all three novels entail death of one kind or another. The roles of Being-towards-Death and Being-beyond-Death in the process of the sublime have been examined here in relation to the development of feminine subjectivity. Death in the case of al-Sa'dāwī's Firdaus, who chooses death over slavery, may be read as being almost aggressively redemptive. Zahra's death in *The Story of Zahra* is far more ambiguous; the unreliability of the narrator invites us to question whether or not she has physically died, and if not, in what sense has she been killed? We have further posited that Kafa's social death in al-Sammān's novel is just as real and complete as bodily death.

Braidotti cites Adam Phillips's conception of a "self-fashioned, self-created death" that is integral to Being (27). The urge towards death as a consummation of Being, or another transition in a long line of transitions, is evident in Firdaus' refusal to accept the commutation of her death sentence. Zahra, after a period of radical indeterminacy, seems to race towards her own death in the second half of her story. Kafa finally has enough, more than enough, and destroys every part of the life she has known. Phillips writes "we are essentially, idiosyncratic suicides, but not from despair, but because it is literally our nature to die" (110).

In the lives of the three heroes, their Being-towards-Death seems to merge with Being-beyond-Death precisely because the death drive and the drive to live are one and the same. "[T]he wish to die is another way to express the desire to live. Not only is there no dialectical tension between Eros and Thanatos, but also the two forces are really just one…." (Braidotti 27).

In all three examples, the death drive and sex are intricately and inextricably bound together. The relationship between *jouissance,* death, sacrifice and the sublime have been remarked upon in the three novels. Braidotti understands death and eroticism as being "connected to the feminine, defined as fluidity, empathy, pleasure, non-closure, a yearning for otherness in the non-appropriative mode, and intensity" (27). Firdaus, Zahra and Kafa each encounter sex and death very differently in the transitions of subjectivity that they undergo. There may be a common element amongst them in which Braidotti calls patterns of becoming, in which we posit that a non-essentialist construction of self takes place in the feminist sublime.

## 5.2.1 The positive in the three deaths

Braidotti emphasizes the processual nature of death, asserting that "it is part of the cycles of becomings, yet another form of inter-connectedness, a vital relationship that links one with other, multiple forces" (17). From her perspective, the continuum or spectrum of Being is unbroken. "Death from the specific and highly restricted viewpoint of the ego is of no significance whatsoever" (17). She cites Ansell Pearson:

A positive, dynamical and processual conception of death, which would release it from an anthropomorphic desire for death (for stasis, for being), speaking instead only of a death that desires (a death that is desire, where desire is construed along the lines of a machine or a machinic assemblage), can only be arrived at by freeing the becoming of death from both mechanism and finalism. (62–63)

Thus, subjectivity can be defined as "flows of patterns of becoming in an unlimited space somewhere between the no longer and the not yet" (Braidotti 17). Death, however one defines it, is not necessarily a finality or even a culmination. It is another stage in the flow of being, part of the autopoiesis of feminine subjectivity. As we have discussed, it plays a key part in the stories of each of the heroes under discussion.

Braidotti draws on Spinoza and Deleuze to call attention to "a logic of positivity" that acknowledges the multiplication "of connections and the wealth of creativity of a self that unfolds in processes of becomings" without resorting to the concept of redemption or transcendence (18). We have discussed the role of transcendence in the masculine sublime, in which the 'other' is overcome or subsumed. Braidotti argues that the logic of positivity in becoming and death is the very opposite of transcendence. While conceptions of transcendence are not repudiated in the feminist sublime, the reinforcement of dualities has no place in it. We briefly discussed Bataille's views on the human need for continuity, which can seemingly be attained through sex, sacrifice or death. This drive towards continuity of being seems to have been an important facet of sublimity for the three heroes we have discussed. The heroes' ontopoiesis included confronting near death experiences (Zahra and Kafa) as well as bodily death (Firdaus and perhaps Zahra) in their pursuit of authentic self, feminine subjectivity and autonomy.

Copjec exposes the fact that although "we moderns are committed to the notion of our own mortality, we nevertheless harbor the secret, inarticulable conviction that we are not mortal" (20). In the past, we could hope to "participate in everlastingness" through the accomplishment of words or deeds that could ring glory through the ages, but the attainment of eternity was impossible. What could be outside time itself? The modern notion, by contrast, is informed by our understanding of that impossibility. This concept gives the acts of all three heroes a resonance and depth that they might not otherwise have achieved. They have realized a kind of immortality that goes beyond simple martyrdom and sainthood, beyond living in the minds of the people who know of them and speak of them, beyond even the power of narrative to convey. The ethical aspects of death without mortality can easily extend into our own minds because of our secret conviction that there is a bridge between "something that no longer exists and something that does not yet exist" (Claude Lefort 270). This liminal stage is included in the feminist sublime.

## 5.2.2 Ethics in the feminist sublime

We have remarked on the strength, and courageously ethical conduct of the heroes in the three novels, even though their acts may be condemned as immoral. Like

Antigone, they act in accordance with their own conception of right and equity to push the boundaries of their bondage, even at the price of personal death. This could be considered profoundly ethical, even as it transgresses against social mores. Mary Walsh notes that "Antigone's death is considered to be a sublime freedom from the moral law that subjects desire to continual negation" (41). Regardless of the consequences, these women act in accordance with the imperative to become.

Braidotti draws on the ethics of Spinoza to formulate an ethics of being which may exemplify the ethics of the feminist sublime because it: "….works by transforming negative into positive passions through the power of the understanding that is no longer indexed upon a phallogocentric set of standards, based on Law and Lack, but is rather unhinged and therefore affective. The task of turning the tide of negativity is an ethical transformative process" (2).

Even while *Woman at Point Zero*, *The Story of Zahra*, and *Night of the First Billion* are deeply negative, they force a reappraisal of women's affectivity and subjectivity outside of the dualisms that entrap. If one accepts that turning the tide of negativity is an ethical transformative process, because it has the potential to better one's own life and that of others, the feminist sublime may offer a rewarding personal practice for reading. Each in their own way, al-Sa'dāwī, al-Shaykh and al-Sammān have articulated an ethics of death in the sublime in the works we reviewed.

## 5.2.3 Value of ambiguity in the feminist sublime

The Arabic women writers in this study use multidimensional meanings in their far-reaching critiques of the effects of patriarchy. The partial being, non-being and refusal of being explored by Firdaus, Zahra, and Kafa are deeply disturbing and suggest both weakness and strength, victimization and the overcoming of domination. Offering many levels of meaning, they also leave an unsettling lack of closure. Maria Walsh points out that many people expect narrative closure and cites Gilberto Perez's "notion of narrative as 'an additive thing that can go on and on without closure'" as something that is anathema to most (72). This lack of closure, which leaves *The Story of Zahra* without an end, with Zahra hovering somewhere between life and death (or perhaps beyond either of those states), and with a consciousness that we cannot quite explain, might also exemplify feminine subjectivity. Although Firdaus may seem to have a definite end, she attains a sort of immortality in a different way, from having told her story to the doctor. Kafa is dead the moment her daughter dies, although she keeps living. All three novels engage the reader in "the continuous transformation of this ambiguity" (Walsh n.pag.). These novels may be read as highlighting the value of ambiguity, not-being and even not-knowing as stages towards or within the feminist sublime.

## 5.3 Questioning the feminist sublime

In writing the heroes' stories, the stories of misery, repression, struggle, and highly ambiguous triumph, the three authors have asked questions about how truth is made for women and how women make their truths. If questions—not answers—are philosophy, they have offered profound questions that lead us not only to the construction of gender and being itself, but also to how truths are constituted. The realities faced by and depicted through Firdaus, Zahra and Kafa cannot be reduced to logical realities. They are creating their own truths. Zamberlin cites David Lapoujade, a "disciple" of Deleuze: "truth is action, transition, creation (rather than representation, conclusion, imitation)" (25). Unfortunately, the action, transition and creation undertaken by our three heroes in defiance of or resistance against patriarchal impositions of truth comes at a high personal price.

In this study, it is accepted that both the attainment and annihilation of selfhood may be a simultaneous, inextricable part of the process of *becoming* in the feminist sublime; the three Arabic women writers have given us the rhizomatic transitions that we need in order to formulate new questions to undertake the dismantling of the binary mental apparatus.

## 5.4 Unmasking the logic of oppression

Is it possible to disassemble the mechanics of the mind that form the basis for othering, and by extension, the very foundation of oppression? If it is possible, this book suggests that thinking about novels such as the three included in this study in terms of the sublime may go some way towards problematizing the deep-seated assumptions that make possible the domination and suppression of humans.

Writing the feminist sublime may be considered not only an essential act of resistance against patriarchal domination, but also one that has the potential to undermine the logic of oppression at a fundamental level. The reconfiguration of the sublime for feminist purposes—that is, for the benefit of men and women—by al-Sa'dāwī, al-Shaykh and al-Sammān has profound ramifications in the development of human thought. We have explored some of the aspects of the sublime in their writing as it relates to revealing the foundation of being, becoming and achieving feminine subjectivity.

Firdaus, Zahra and Kafa are all betrayed by the dualisms enacted out of their own minds and the minds of others. In different ways, they are led or lead themselves into formlessness, non-being and the in-between states that are, by their very nature, outside the limitations of dualism. This form of protest against the fundamental mechanism of their suppression is achieved only through traumatic incidents. Zahra seems to experience this in-betweenness as indeterminacy or what Žižek calls the "will-less will" (qtd. in Jagodzinski 1-24). Firdaus takes strong, willful action, yet she too undergoes in-betweenness repeatedly. Her becomingness is sharply and painfully curtailed. Kafa, who caricatures stereotypical upper-class prostitutes, finds that the restrictions placed on her by a patriarchal socio-economic structure founded on dualisms are impossible to escape. Like those of Firdaus and Zahra, Kafa's explorations of in-betweenness and becoming are futile. Or are they?

In a comparison of Žižek and Deleuze, Jan Jagodzinski quotes Deleuze's conception of how we are cut into segments, lines cut across our consciousness, restricting us and blinding us, from *Dialogues*: "The segments depend on binary machines, diverse according to need. Binary machines of social classes, sexes, man-female, ages, child-adult, races, white-black, of private and public sectors, of subjectivations, from here-not, from here" (156).

However, such polarity can be destroyed, "not because they combine to become one, but because they always introduce a 'third that comes from elsewhere and upsets the binarity of the two'" (Zamberlin 21). What is this third, and how can we invite it to appear? This researcher suggests that the writings of al-Sa'dāwī, al-Shaykh and al-Sammān seen through the lens of the sublime may open the door for the third to appear. It is not a merging of the initial two, but a new and different kind of being and thinking. This "third" way of being or thinking undermines our segmentation, the "binary machines" we construct and which have been constructed for us in order to keep us as we are and the world as it is. At the outset, it was hoped that this study might encourage readers to think through the mental processes of patriarchal oppression, and so eventually weaken or destroy them, making way for non-binary thinking that does not 'other' either men or women. It is hoped that this possibility now seems more genuine than it may have seemed at the beginning of this study.

Zamberlin cites Jean Wahl to explain the possibility of reaching an emptiness beyond polarizing dualities in order to create a better world. In Wahl's case, he spoke of achieving the point beyond binaries through art. The feminist sublime in Arabic women's writing is non-adversarial in its approach, and may well be able to reach that empty space beyond the snare of binary thinking. Wahl's notion of moving from "antithesis toward ecstasy," the space beyond right/wrong, man/woman, etc., is relevant to the writing of all three authors we have discussed. According to the *Merriam-Webster Dictionary*, ecstasy means "out of or beyond stasis." The three women heroes encountered and went beyond stasis, variously defined as death, void, formlessness, or radical passivity. This researcher believes that seeking to better understand feminine subjectivity through the feminist sublime as we have been discussing can yield pragmatic insights. Art, such as these three novels, can be effective in accomplishing change because art "speaks to the whole being," leads us to the imperceptible, articulates problems rather than solutions, makes us uncomfortable with accepted truths, communicates the fullness of human existence, "and transmits existential realities that reason based disciplines efface, reduce or simply can't account for" (Wahl 47). That is, the ability of such writing as we have examined in this study to transcend or otherwise exceed binary machines. It is worthwhile to quote Wahl on the wholeness that may be achieved through art: "[W]e experience a fullness of being, we no longer separate the inner and the outer, the infinite and the finite, and the unceasing dialogue comes to its conclusion, in silence" (324). This absence of separation may be at the heart of the sublime experience. Perhaps in the feminist sublime, we can reformulate the ontological foundations of being and subjectivity.

The sublime as a framework may be capable of being disassociated from Western culture, and thus may avoid the perceived or actual stigma of being a Western import and the politicized pigeonhole to which that may lead. Moreover, a sublime reading may be concerned with ethics, without necessarily being morally judgmental; at the least, it may offer ways to understand differing moralities. Further, such a reading offers an inclusive quality, which does not try to suppress or homogenize differences, whether gender, sexual orientation, ethnic, religious, or any other. Finally, a sublime reading does not, by its nature, necessarily favor one philosophy or mode of thought over another, so that it may be adapted to the particular situations of those who have been minoritized, colonized or otherwise oppressed. It is also suggested that the women who have undergone the experiences of the feminist sublime in these three novels have demonstrated strength and purpose; they have borne any amount of pain necessary in order to achieve their objective of self-realization and self-expression. It is hoped that the feminist sublime offers a space in which to recognize and negotiate differences and resist patriarchic structures without simultaneously reinforcing them.

# Bibliography

Abu-Haidar, Faridah. A Voice from Iraq: The Fiction of Alia Mamdouh. *Women: A Cultural Review* 9.3 (1998): pp. 305–11. Print.

Abu-Lughod, Lila. The Marriage of Feminism and Islamism in Egypt: Selective Repudiation as a Dynamic of Postcolonial Cultural Politics. In *Remaking Women: Feminism and Modernity in the Middle East* Ed. Lila Abu-Lughod. Princeton: Princeton University Press, 1998. Print.

Accad, Evelyne. *Sexuality and War: Literary Masks of the Middle East.* New York: New York University Press, 1990. Print.

—. Gender and Violence in Lebanese War Novels. *From Patriarchy to Empowerment: Women's Participation, Movements, and Rights in the Middle East, North Africa and South Asia.* Syracuse: Syracuse University Press, 2007: pp. 293-310. Print.

Adams, A. M. Writing Self, Writing Nation: Imagined Geographies in the Fiction of Hanan al-Shaykh. *Tulsa Studies in Women's Literature, Women Writing Across the World* 20.2 (2001): pp. 201-216. Print.

Ahmed, Leila. Arab Culture and Writing Women's Bodies. *Gender Issues* 9.1 (1989): pp. 41-55. Print.

Afaki, Abdul Rahim. Historicality of Linguistic Signs: Limits of Fruitfulness of Western Hermeneutics, in Interpreting the Transformation of Arab Tradition. In *Timing and Temporality in Islamic Philosophy and Phenomenology of Life.* Vol. 3. Eds. Anna-Teresa Tymieniecka, Gholam Reza A'awani, Nader el-Bizri. Dordrecht, The Netherlands: Springer, 2007: pp. 195-219. Print.

Agnew, Lois. The Classical Period. In *The Present State of Scholarship in the History of Rhetoric: A Twenty-first Century Guide.* 3rd ed. Missouri: University of Missouri, 2010: pp. 7-25. Print.

Aldea, Eva. *Magical Realism and Deleuze: The Indiscernibility of Difference in Postcolonial Literature.* London and NYC: Continuum Publishing, 2010. Print.

Alexandrov, Vladimir. The Otherworld in *Invitation to a Beheading*. In *Nabokov's Invitation to a Beheading: A Critical Companion*. Ed. Julian W Connolly. Llinois: Northwestern University Press, 1997. Print.

Al-Id, Yumna. Lebanon. *Arab Women Writers: A Critical Reference Guide 1873-1999*. Cairo: The American University in Cairo Press, 2008: pp. 13-59. Print.

Allen, Prudence, R.S.M. *The Concept of Woman: The Aristotelian Revolution, 750 BC – AD 1250*. Montreal and London: Eden Press, 1985. Print.

Allen, Roger M.A. MESA Presidential Address 2010: A Translator's Tale. *Review of Middle East Studies* 45.1 (2011): pp. 3-18. Web. https://library.villanova.edu/Find/Summon/Record?id=FETCH-jstor_primary_10_2307_230571001 (Last accessed 2 June 2013)

—. PROTA: The Project for the Translation of Arabic. *Middle East Studies Association Bulletin* 28.2, pp. 165-168. 1994. Print.

—. *An Introduction to Arabic Literature. Cambridge*: Cambridge University Press, 2000. Print.

—. *The Arabic Novel: An Historical and Critical Introduction*. Syracuse: Syracuse University Press, 1995. Print.

—. "The Mature Arabic Novel Outside Europe." In *Modern Arabic Literature*. Ed. M.M. Badawi. Cambridge: Cambridge University Press, pp. 192-222. 1992. Print.

—. *The Arabic Novel: An Historical and Critical Introduction*. 2nd Ed. Syracuse, New York: Syracuse University Press, 1995. Print.

—. (Ed). *Essays in Arabic Literary Biography: 1850-1950*. Harrassowitz: 2010. Print.

Al-Masri, Khaled M. *Telling Stories of Pain: Women Writing Gender, Sexuality and Violence in the Novel of the Lebanese Civil War*. Doctoral thesis, University of Michigan, 2010. Web. ProQuest, UMI Dissertation Publishing. Available on web: http://udini.proquest.com/view/telling-stories-of-pain-women-goid:762209963/ (Last accessed 2 June 2013).

Al-Otaibi, Fahad M. "Towards a Contrapuntal Reading of History: Orientalism and the Ancient Near East." *J. King Saud Univ.*, Vol. 19, *Arts* (2), pp. 55-66. Riyadh. 2006. Print.

Al-Shaykh, Hanan. *The Story of Zahra*. Trans. Peter Ford. New York: Anchor Books, 1995. Print.

Al-Shaykh, Hanan. The New Shahrazad. *Sweet Briar College World Writers Series* Mar 15 2000: (n. pag.). Web. http://gos.sbc.edu/a/al-Shaykh.htm (Last accessed 19 May 2012).

Amireh, Amal. Publishing in the West: Problems and Prospects for Arab Women Writers. *Al-Jadid: A Record of Arab Culture and the Arts* 2.10 (1996): (n. pag.) Web. http://www.aljadid.com/features/0210amireh.html (Last accessed 10 December 2012).

*American Heritage Dictionary of the English Language*. 4th ed. Boston: Houghton Mifflin Harcourt Company, 2000. Print.

Asad, T. *Formations of the Secular: Christianity, Islam, Modernity*. Stanford: Stanford University Press, 2003. Print.

—. *On Suicide Bombing*. New York: Columbia University Press, 2007. Print.

—. Afterword: From the History of Colonial Anthropology to the Anthropology of Western Hegemony. In *Colonial Situations: Essays on the Contextualization of Ethnographic Knowledge*. Ed. G. W. Stocking Jr. Madison: University of Wisconsin Press, 1993: pp. 314-324. Print.

—. Europe against Islam: Islam in Europe. *The Muslim World* 87.2, 183-195. 1997. Print.

Assagioli, Roberto. *Transpersonal Development: The Dimension Beyond Psychosynthesis*. Findhorn, Scotland: InnerWay Productions, 2007. Print.

Azadpur, Mohammad. *Reason Unbound: On Spiritual Practice in Islamic Peripatetic Philosophy*. New York: SUNY Press, 2011. Print.

—. The Sublime Visions of Philosophy: Fundamental Ontology and the Imaginal World. In *Islamic Philosophy and Occidental Phenomenology on the Perennial Issue of Microcosm and Macrocosm*. Ed. A.-T. Tymieniecka. Dordrecht, The Netherlands: Springer, 2006: pp. 113-126. Print.

Badran, Margot, and miriam cooke. Introduction. *Opening the Gate: An Anthology of Arab Feminist Writing*. 2nd ed. Ed. Badran and Cooke. Indiana: Indiana University Press, 2004. pp. xxv-xlvii. Print.

Bakhtin, Mikhail. *Rabelais and His World*. Bloomington, IN: Indiana University Press, 2009. Print.

Ball, John Clement. *Imagining London: Postcolonial Fiction and the Transnational Metropolis*. Toronto: University of Toronto Press, 2004. Print.

Ballif, Michelle. Re/Dressing Histories: Or, On Recovering Figures Who Have Been Laid Bare by Our Gaze. *Rhetoric Society Quarterly* 22.1 (1992): pp. 91–99. Print.

Bassnett, Susan. *Translation Studies*. 3rd ed. London: Routledge, 2002 Print.

Bassnett, Susan and Lefevere, Andre, eds. *Constructing Cultures: Essays on Literary Translation*. Bristol, PA: Multilingual Matters Ltd, 1998. Print.

Battaille, Georges. *Death and Sensuality: A Study of Eroticism and the Taboo*. Trans. Mary Dalwood. New York: Walker & Co., 1962. Print.

Ben-Porat, Ziva. Method in Madness: Notes on the Structure of Parody, Based on MAD TV Satires. *Poetics Today* 1.1/2 (1979): (no pag.) Web. http://poeticstoday.dukejournals.org/content/22/1/25.abstract (Last accessed 23 May 2013)

Bizzell, Patricia. Opportunities for Feminist Research in the History of Rhetoric. *Rhetoric Review* 11.1 (1992): pp. 50-58. Print.

Boardman, J. *The Greeks Overseas*. London: Thames and Hudson, 1999. Print.

Booth, Marilyn. *May Her Likes Be Multiplied: Biography and Gender Politics in Egypt*. Berkeley: University of California Press, 2001. Print.

—. Exemplary Lives, Feminist Aspirations: Zaynab Fawwāz and the Arabic Biographical Tradition. *Journal of Arabic Literature* 26; 1/2. 1995.pp 120-146. Print.

Boyer, P. The Naturalness of Religion: A Cognitive Theory of Religion. Berkeley, CA: University of California Press, 1994. Print.

Braidotti, Rosi. The Ethics of Becoming Imperceptible. In *Deleuze and Philosophy*. Ed. Constantin Boundas. Edinburgh: Edinburgh University Press, 2006: pp. 133-159. Print.

Brans, Jo. Using What You're Given. In *Waltzing Again: New and Selected Conversations with Margaret Atwood*. Ed. Earl G. Ingersoll. Princeton, NJ: Ontario Review Press, 2006: pp. 79-89. Print.

Brunner, Rainer and Werner Ende. *The Twelver Shia in Modern Times: Religious Culture & Political Culture*. Leiden: Brill, 2000. Print.

Büchler, Alexandra, Alice Guthrie, Barbora Černá and Michal Karas. *Literature Across Frontiers: Literary translation from Arabic into English in the United Kingdom and Ireland, 1990-2010*. Mercator Institute for Media, Languages and Culture, Aberystwyth University, Wales, UK. 2011. Web. http://www.translationstudiesportal.org/publications/entry/literary_translation_from_arabic_into_english_in_the_united_kingdom_and_ire (Last accessed 6 June 2013)

Burke, Edmund. *Philosophical Enquiry into the Origin of Our Ideas of the Sublime and the Beautiful.* 1757. Web. http://www.bartleby.com/24/2/ (Last accessed 2 June 2013)

Burkert, W. *The Orientalizing Revolution.* Trans. W. Burkert. London: Harvard University Press, 1992. Print.

Butz, D. and Berg, L.D. Paradoxical Space: Geography, Men, and Duppy Feminism. In *Feminist Geography in Practice Research and Methods.* Ed. Pamela Moss. Oxford: Blackwell Publishers Ltd, 2002: pp. 87-102. Print.

Campbell, Joseph. *Myths to Live By.* New York City: Bantam Books, 1973. Print.

Camus, Albert. *An Absurd Reasoning.* In *The Myth of Sisyphus: And Other Essays* Trans. Justin O'Brien. 1955, Reissue edition, New York: Vintage Books, 1991. Print.

Cantor, Jennifer. Vision and Virtue in Psychoanalysis and Buddhism: Anatta and Its Implications for Social Responsibility. *Psychoanalytic Inquiry: A Topical Journal for Mental Health Professionals* 28:5 (2008): pp. 532-540. Web. http://www.tandfonline.com/doi/full/10.1080/07351690802228831#.UbUB9diY52E (Last accessed 2 June 2013)

Chatman, Seymour. Parody and Style. *Poetics Today* 22.1 (2001) (n. pag.) DukeUniversityPress.Web.http://poeticstoday.dukejournals.org/content/22/1/25 (Last accessed 2 June 2013)

Clark, R.T. Rundle. *Myth and Symbol in Ancient Egypt.* London: Thames & Hudson, 1959. Print.

Cochran, Peter. Longinus, Sappho's Ode, and the Question of Sublimity. *Revue de l'Université de Moncton* 2005: pp. 219-232. Print.

—. Francis Cohen, Don Juan, and Casti. *Romanticism* 4. (1998): pp. 120-124. Print.

Cook, Kathleen C. Sexual Inequality in Aristotle's Theories. In *Feminism and Ancient Philosophy.* Ed. Julie Ward. New York: Routledge, 1996. Print.

Cooke, Miriam. *War's Other Voices: Women Writers on the Lebenese Civil War.* New York: Cambridge University Press, 1996. Print.

Connell, R.W. *Masculinities.* Berkeley: University of California Press, 2005.

Corbin, Henry. *Alone with the Alone: Creative Imagination in the Sufism of Ibn 'Arabi.* Princeton: Mythos, Princeton University Press, 1997. Print.

Cowling, Faith. The Pioneers: Ghada Samman. *For'em Magazine Current Social and Political Issues with a Gender Twist.* September 30, 2011: (n.pag.) Web. http://foremmagazine.wordpress.com/2011/09/30/the-pioneers-ghada-samman/ (Last accessed 27 May 2013).

Cronin, Michael. Altered States: Translation and Minority Languages. *TTR: Traduction, Terminologie, Redaction* 8.1 (1995): pp. 85-103. Web. http://id.erudit.org/iderudit/037198ar (Last accessed 2 June 2013).

Davis, A. *Women, Race, and Class.* New York: Random House, 1981. Print.

Deleuze, Gilles and Claire Parnet. *Dialogues.* Paris: Flammarion, 1996. Print.

Dresner, Zita. Women's Humor. In *Humor in America. A Research Guide to Genres and Topics.* Ed. Lawrence E. Mintz. Westport, CT: Greenwood, 1988: pp. 137-161. Print.

Dufourmantelle, Anne. *Blind Date: Sex and Philosophy.* Trans. Catherine Porter. Chicago: University of Illinois Press, 2007. Print.

El-Aswad, el-Sayed. *Religion and Folk Cosmology: Scenarios of the Visible and Invisible in Rural Egypt.* Westport, CT: Praeger, 2002. Print.

Eisenhower, Dwight D. *Public Papers of the Presidents, Dwight D. Eisenhowe.* 1960: pp. 1035-1040. Web. http://quod.lib.umich.edu/p/ppotpus?key=title;page=browse;value=d (Last accessed 2 June 2013).

El Koudia, Jilali, Roger Allen, and Hasan El-Shamy. *Moroccan Folktales (Middle East Literature in Translation).* Syracuse, New York: Syracuse University Press, 2003. Print.

El Saadawi. *The Essential Nawal El Saadawi: A Reader.* Ed. Adele Newson-Horst. New York: Palgrave Macmillan, 2010. Print.

—. *Woman at Point Zero.* 2$^{nd}$ ed. Trans. Sherif Hetata. London: Zed Books, 2007.

—. *The Circling Song.* Trans. Marilyn Booth. London: Zed Books, 1989.

El Saddah, Hoda. Egypt. *Arab Women Writers: A Critical Reference Guide 1873-1999.* Cairo: The American University in Cairo Press. 2008. pp 98-161. Print.

El-Shamy, Hasan M. *Folk Traditions of the Arab World: A Guide to Motif Classification.* 2 vols. Bloomington: Indiana University Press, 1995. Print.

*Encyclopedia Britannica.* Sections: Heidegger and Heidegger's hermeneutic phenomenology. Web. http://www.britannica.com/EBchecked/topic/259513/Martin-Heidegger (Last accessed 2 June 2013).

Ettinger, Bracha L. Matrix and Metramorphosis. *Differences. Special Issue: Trouble in the Archives.* Ed. Griselda Pollock. 4. (1992): pp. 176-208. Print.

Fayad, Mona. Reinscribing Identity: Nation and community in Arab women's writing. *College Literature.* 22.1 (1995): pp.147-160. Third World Women's Inscriptions. Web. http://www.jstor.org/discover/10.2307/25112170?uid=3739560&uid=4580699347&uid=2129&uid=2&uid=70&uid=3&uid=3739256&uid=60&sid=21102087086163 (Last accessed 27 May 2013)

Faris, Wendy B. *Ordinary Enchantments: Magical Realism and the Remystification of Narrative.* Nashville, TN: Vanderbilt University Press, 2004. Print.

Fido, Elaine Savory. Mother / lands: Self and Separation in the work of Buchi Emecheta, Bessie Head and Jean Rhys. In *Motherlands: Black Women's Writing from Africa, the Caribbean and South Asia.* Ed. Susheila Nasta. London: The Women's Press, 1991: pp. 330-50.

Fletcher, Angus. *Allegory: The Theory of a Symbolic Mode.* 3rd ed. Ithaca: Cornell University Press, 1982. Print.

Fraiman, Susan. *Unbecoming Women: British Women Writers and the Novel of Development.* New York: Columbia University Press, 1993. Print.

Foss, Sonja K. and Cindy L. Griffin. Beyond Persuasion: A Proposal for an Invitational Rhetoric. *Communication Monographs.* 62. (1995): pp. 1-19. Web. http://www.sonjafoss.com/html/Foss21.pdf (Last accessed 27 May 2013).

Freeman, Barbara. *The Feminine Sublime: Gender and Excess in Women's Fiction.* Berkeley: University of California Press, 1997. Print.

Freud, S. The Uncanny. *The Standard Edition of the Complete Psychological Works of Sigmund Freud, Volume XVII (1917-1919): An Infantile Neurosis and Other Works*, pp. 217-256. 1919. Print.

Gadamer, Hans Georg. *Wahrheit und Methode (Truth and Method)* trans. G. Barden and W.G. Doerpel. New York: Crossroad, 1975. Print.

Gaillet, Lynee Lewis and Winifred Bryan Horner, eds. *The Present State of Scholarship in the History of Rhetoric: A Twenty-first Century Guide*. 3rd ed. Colombia, MO: University of Missouri, 2010. Print.

Gaines, Robert N. Aristotle's Rhetoric and the Contemporary Arts of Practical Discourse. In *Rereading Aristotle's Rhetoric*. Eds. Alan G. Gross and Arthur E. Walzer. Carbondale, IL: Southern Illinois University, 2000. Print.

Garry, Jane and Hasan M. El-Shamy. *Archetypes And Motifs In Folklore And Literature: A Handbook*. M.E. Sharpe. 2004. Print.

Genette, Gerard. *Narrative Discourse: An Essay in Method*, trans. Jane E. Lewin. Ithaca: Cornell University Press, 1980.

Ghandour, Sabah. Hanan al-Shaykh's Hikayat Zahra: a Counter-Narrative and a Counter-History in *Intersections: Gender, Nation, and Community in Arab Women's Novels*. Lisa Suhair Majaj, Paula Wanda Sundeman, and Therese Saliba, eds. Syracuse, NY: Syracuse University Press, 2002: pp. 231-52. Print.

Glenn, Cheryl. Sex, Lies, and Manuscript: Refiguring Aspasia in the History of Rhetoric. *College Composition and Communication*. 45.2 (1994): pp. 180-199. Print.

Gregson, Ian. *Character and Satire in Post-War Fiction*. London: Continuum, 2006.

Grosz, Elizabeth. *Sexual Subversions*. Sydney: Allen & Unwin, 1989. Print.

Guerlac, Suzanne. Longinus and the Subject of the Sublime. *New Literary History. The Sublime and the Beautiful: Reconsiderations.* 16.2 (1985): pp. 275-289

Guven, Ferit. *Madness and Death in Philosophy (SUNY Series in Contemporary Continental Philosophy)*. New York: State University of New York Press, 2006.

Hadidi, Subhi and Iman al-Qadi. Syria. *Arab Women Writers: A Critical Reference Guide 1873-1999*. The American University in Cairo Press: Cairo. 2008. pp.60-97. Print.

Hall, Manly Palmer. *The Secret Teachings of All Ages: An Encyclopedic Outline of Masonic, Hermetic, Qabbalistic and Rosicrucian Symbolical Philosophy*. Los Angeles: Forgotten Books, 2008. Print.

Hall, Stuart. Political Belonging in a World of Multiple Identities. *Conceiving Cosmopolitanism: Theory, Context, and Practice*. Eds. Steven Vertovec and Robin Cohen. Oxford: Oxford University Press, 2002. Print.

Haney, Kathleen. Lukacs, Georg. *The Theory of the Novel*. London: The Merlin Press Ltd. 1978. Print.

Harbawi, Semia. Narrativising Betrayal in Hanan al-Shaykh's The Story of Zahra. *Arabesques Cultures and Dialogues*. 2.4 (2007): (n. pag.). Web. http://www.arabesques-editions.com/journal/books_reviews/01388075.html (Last accessed 2 Jun 2013).

Heidegger, Martin. *Being and Time*. Trans. John Macquarie and Edward Robinson. Oxford: Basil Blackwell, 1988. Print.

Heider, Karl G. The Rashomon Effect: When Ethnographers Disagree. *American Anthropologist*, New Series, 90.1 (1988): pp. 73-81. Print.

Hick, John. *An Interpretation of Religion: Human Responses to the Transcendent* 2$^{nd}$ ed. London: Yale University Press, 2005. Print.

Hirsh, Marianne. *The Mother / Daughter Plot: Narrative, Psychoanalysis, Feminism*. New York City: John Wiley & Sons, 1989. Print.

Hocart, A.M. The Legacy to Modern Egypt In *The Legacy of Egypt*. Ed. A.M. Hocart. London: Oxford University Press, 1942: pp. 369–469. Print.

Hughes, Micah A. Mr. Representations of Identity in Three Modern Arabic Novels. *Colonial Academic Alliance Undergraduate Research Journal* 2.5 (2011): pp. 1-32. Web. http://scholarworks.gsu.edu/caaurj/vol2/iss1/5 (Last accessed 23 May 2013).

Hutcheon, Linda. *A Theory of Parody: The Teachings of Twentieth-Century Art Forms*. New York: Methuen, 1985. Print.

—. Parody without Ridicule: Observations on Modern Literary Parody. *Canadian Review of Comparative Literature/Revue Canadienne de Littérature Comparée* 5. (1978): pp. 201-211. Print.

Irigaray, Luce. *I love to You: Sketch for a Felicity within History*. Trans. Alison Martin. New York: Routledge, 1996. Print.

—. *An Ethics of Sexual Difference*. trans. Carolyn Burke & Gillian C. Gill. Ithaca: Cornell University Press, 1993. Print.

—. *Speculum of the Other Woman*. Trans. Gillian C. Gill. Ithaca: Cornell University Press, 1985. Print.

Jagodzinski, Jan. Struggling with Žižek's Ideology: The Deleuzian Complaint, Or, Why is Žižek a Disguised Deleuzian in Denial? *International Jounral of Žižek Studies* 4.1 (2010): pp. 1-24 Web. http://zizekstudies.org/index.php/ijzs/ issue/view/17 (Last accessed 2 June 2013).

Jarratt, Susan C. *Rereading the Sophists: Classical Rhetoric Refigured*. Carbondale, IL: Southern Illinois University Press, 1991. Print.

Johnson, Adrian. The Exception and the Rule: Judith Butler's "Antigone's Claim." *Continental Philosophy Review* 35.4 (2002): pp. 425-449. Print.

Jung, C.G. *Man and His Symbols*. New York: Dell Publishing, 1978 [1964 reprint]. Print.

—. *Collected Works of C.G. Jung*, Vol. 9 (Part 1): *Archetypes and the Collective Unconscious*. Ed. and trans. Gerhard Adler and R.F.C. Hull. Princeton, NJ: Princeton University Press, 1981. Print.

—. "Approaching the Unconscious." In *Man and His Symbols*. Eds. Carl Jung, M.L. von Franz, Joseph, Henderson, Jolande Jacobi, and Aniela Jaffe. Garden City, NY: Doubleday, 1964: pp. 18–103. Print.

Kant, Immanuel. *The Critique of Pure Reason*. Translated by Miller D. Meikeljohn. London: Everyman, 1993 [1787]. Print.

Kaplan, Robert. *The Nothing that Is: The Natural History of Zero*. USA: Oxford University Press, 2000. Print.

Keen, Sam. The Golden Mean of Roberto Assagioli in *Psychology Today,* Dec.1974. Web. http://samkeen.com/interviews-by-sam/interviews-by-sam/the-golden-mean-of-roberto-assagioli/ (Last accessed 5 June 2013).

Khanna, Madhu. *Yantra: The Tantric Symbol of Cosmic Unity*. Rochester, VT: Inner Traditions. 2003. Print.

Kenney, Mary Ann. *Mysterious Chrysalis: A Phenomenological Study of Personal Transformation.* Diss. Pacifica Graduate Institute, California. 2008.Web. https://library.villanova.edu/Find/Summon/Record?id=FETCH-proquest_dll_14834732811 (Last accessed 11 Feb 2013).

Knight, Charles A. *The Literature of Satire*. Cambridge: Cambridge University Press, 2004. Print.

Knowles, John. Subversive Discourses in Hanan Al-Shaykh; Pushing out the boundaries of Arab feminism in the novel. *Contemporary Women's Issues* 10 (1997): pp. 15-20. Print.

Kochin, Michael S. *Gender and Rhetoric in Plato's Political Thought*. Cambridge: Cambridge University Press, 2002. Print.

Kristeva, Julia. *Powers of Horror: An Essay on Abjection.* Translated by Leon S. Roudiez. New York: Columbia University Press, 1982. Print.

Lerner, Gerda. *The Creation of Feminist Consciousness: From the Middle Ages to Eighteen-seventy.* London: Oxford University Press, 1994. Print.

Lacan, Jacques. *Seminar VII. The Ethics of Psychoanalysis.* W. W. Norton & Company, 1997. Print.

Lanza, Robert. Biocentrism: Where Did The Universe Come From? Web. http://www.robertlanzabiocentrism.com/where-did-the-universe-come-(Last accessed 2 June 2013).

Lefort, Claude. *Democracy and Political Theory.* Trans. David Macey. Cambridge: Polity Press, 1988: pp. 256-281. Print.

Lindemans, Micha F. *Encyclopedia Mythica.* Encyclopedia Mythica Online. 1997. Web. http://www.pantheon.org/ (Last accessed 23 May 2013).

Lionnet, Françoise. *Postcolonial Representations: Women, Literature, Identity.* Ithaca: Cornell University Press, 1995. Print.

Longinus. *On Great Writing (On the Sublime).* Trans G. M. A. Grube. Indianapolis & Cambridge: Hackett, 1991. Print.

Lyotard, Jean-François. Answering the Question: What is Postmodernism? Trans. Régis Durand. *The Postmodern Condition: A Report on Knowledge.* Manchester: Machester University Press, 1984: pp. 71-82. Print.

—. Lyotard, Jean-François. *Political Writings.* Trans. Bill Readings and Kevin Paul Geiman. Minneapolis: University of Minnesota Press, 1993. Print.

Mahmood, S. *The Politics of Piety - The Islamic Reformation and the Feminist Subject.* Princeton: Princeton University Press, 2004. Print.

Maier, Carol. Toward a Theoretical Practice for Cross-Cultural Translation. In *Between Languages and Cultures: Translation and Cross-Cultural Texts.* Anuradha Dingwaney and Carol Maier, eds. University of Pittsburgh Press, 1996: pp. 21-38. Print.

Mairs, Nancy. *Voice Lessons: On Becoming a (Woman) Writer.* Boston: Beacon Press, 1997. Print.

Majaj, Lisa Suhair, Paula Wanda Sundeman, and Therese Saliba. *Intersections: Gender, Nation, and Community in Arab Women's Novels.* New York: Syracuse University Press, 2002.

Malti-Douglas, Fedwa. *Men, Women, and God(s): Nawal El Saadawi and Arab Feminist Poetics.* Berkeley: University of California Press. 1995. Print.

Mann, Bonnie. *Women's Liberation and the Sublime: Feminism, Postmodernism Environment (Studies in Feminist Philosophy).* New York: Oxford University Press, 2006. Print.

Margolis, Jonathan. *O: The Intimate History of the Orgasm.* New York: Grove Press, 2004. Print.

Marroum, Marianne Rita. *Life in Chaos in Works of El-Sheikh and Chedid.* UMI Dissertation Information Service, 1993. Print.

Mbembe, Achille. Necropolitics. *Public Culture* 15.1 (2003): pp. 11–40. Durham: Duke University Press. Print.

McCrudden, M. T., and Schraw, G. Relevance and Goal-focusing in Text Processing. *Educational Psychology Review.* 19.2 (2007): pp. 113–139. Print.

McGowan, John. *Postmodernism and Its Critics.* Ithaca: Cornell University Press, 1991. Print.

McManus, I.C. Symmetry and Asymmetry in Aesthetics and the Arts. *European Review.* 13.2 (2005): pp. 157–180. Print.

*Merriam-Webster Dictionary.* Dasein. Web. http://www.merriam-webster.com/dictionary/dasein (Last access 27 May 2013)

Merton, Thomas. *Symbolism: Communication or Communion?* 1965. Web. http://merton.org/Research/Manuscripts/manu.aspx?id=3517 (Last accessed 23 May 2013)

Mies, M. Towards a Methodology for Feminist Research. *Theories of Women's Studies.* Eds. G. Bowles and R. Duelli Klein. London: Routledge & Kegan Paul, 1983. Print.

— Women's research or feminist research? The debate surrounding feminist science and methodology. In *Beyond Methodology: Feminist Scholarship as Lived Research.* Eds. M. M. Fonow and J. A. Cook. Bloomington: Indiana University Press, 1991. Print.

Miller, Paul Allen. Lacan's Antigone: The Sublime Object and the Ethics of Interpretation. *Phoenix,* Published by Classical Association of Canada. 61.1/2 (2007): pp. 1-14. Print.

Mirikitani, J., ed. *Third World Women.* San Francisco: Third World Communications, 1973. Print.

Moraga, C. and Anzaldúa, G., eds. *This Bridge Called My Back: Writings by Radical Women of Color.* Watertown, MA: Persephone, 1981. Print.

Moss, Pamela. A Bodily Notion of Research: Power, Difference, and Specificity in Feminist Methodology. In *A Companion to Feminist Geography.* Eds. Lise Nelson and Joni Seager. Oxford: Blackwell Publishing, 2005: pp. 41-59. Print.

Nabokov's interview 6. *Wisconsin Studies in Contemporary Literature.* VIII;2 (1967): (n. pag.). Web. http://lib.ru/NABOKOW/Inter06.txt_with-big-pictures.html (Last accessed 2 June 2013)

Nietzsche, Friedrich. *The Birth of Tragedy Out of the Spirit of Music.* Trans. Ian Johnston. Nanaimo, BC: Vancouver Island University. 2009. [1872] Web.http://www.richerresourcespublications.com/E-Books/philosophic_titles/Nietzsche/Birth%20of%20Tragedy-excerpt.pdf (Last accessed 23 May 2013)

Newton, K. M., ed. *Twentieth Century Literary Theory: A Reader.* Basingstoke: Macmillan Education, 1988. Print.

Obrist, Hans Ulrich. In Conversation with Nawal El Saadawi. *E-flux.* Journal 42. 2013. Web. http://www.e-flux.com/journal/in-conversation-with-nawal-el-saadawi/ (Last accessed 5 June 2013).

O'Connor, Erin. Preface for a Post-Postcolonial Criticism. *Victorian Studies.* 45.2 (2003): pp. 217-246. Print.

O'Grady, Kathleen. Theorizing—Feminism and Postmodernity: A Conversation with Linda Hutcheon. *Rampike* 9.2 (1998): pp. 20-22. Web. http://oldsite.english.ucsb. edu/ faculty/ayliu/research/grady-hutcheon.html (Last accessed 2 June 2013)

O'Keefe, Juliet. Woman at Point Zero: The Vision of Nawal El Saadawi. *Dissent Magazine* Democratiya 15. 2008. Web. http://www.academia.edu/1584371/ Une_si_longue_presence_comment_le_monde_arabe_a_perdu_ses_Juifs_ 1947-1967 (Last accessed 21 May 2013)

Ong, Walter J. Foreward to the 1990 Edition. In *The Present State of Scholarship in Historical and Contemporary Rhetoric: A Twenty-first Century Guide*. Ed. Winifred B. Horner. Missouri: University of Missouri, 2010: pp. 1-6 Print.

Phillips, Adam. *Darwin's Worms*. London: Faber & Faber, 1999. Print.

Pollock, Griselda. Mother Trouble: The Maternal-Feminine in Phallic and Feminist Theory in Relation to Bracha Ettinger's Elaboration of Matrixial Ethics/Aesthetics. *Studies in the Maternal* 1.1 (2009): pp. 1-31 Web. www.mamsie.bbk.ac.uk/back_issues/issue_one/GriseldaPollock.pdf (Last accessed 27 May 2013)

Porter, James. *The Invention of Dionysus: An Essay on The Birth of Tragedy*. Palo Alto, CA: Stanford University Press, 2000. Print.

Purdy, Susan. *Comedy. The Mastery of Discourse*. Hemel Hempstead: Harvester Wheatsheaf, 1993. Print.

Rastegar, Kamran. Literary *Modernity between the Middle East and Europe: Textual transactions in nineteenth-century Arabic, English, and Persian literatures.* London and New York: Routledge. 2007. Print.

Ratcliffe, Krista. The Twentieth and Twenty-first Centuries. In *The Present State of Scholarship in the History of Rhetoric: A Twenty-first Century Guide*. 3rd ed. Ed. Winifred B. Horner. Columbia, MO: University of Missouri Press, 2010: pp. 185-212. Print.

Rogers, G. M. Multiculturalism and the Foundations of Western Civilization. In *Black Athena Revisited*. Ed. G.M. Rogers. London: The University of North Carolina Press, 1996. Print.

Rogers, Robert. *A Psychoanalytic Study of the Double in Literature*. Detroit: Wayne State University Press, 1970. Print.

Rosaldo, Renato. Ideology, Place, and People without Culture. *Cultural Anthropology* 3.1 (1988): pp. 77-87.

Rumi, Mevlana Jalalu-'d-din Muhammad. *Masnavi i Ma'navi - Teachings of Rumi: The Spiritual Couplets of Maulana Jalalu-'d-din Muhammad i Rumi*. Trans and abridged E.H. Whinfield. Ames, IA: Omphaloskepsis, 2001. Print.

Said, Edward W. *Representations of the Intellectual: The 1993 Reith Lectures*. New York: Vintage Books, 1996. Print.

—. *Orientalism*. New York: Vintage; 1st Vintage Books, 1979. Print.

—. *The World, the Text, and the Critic*. London: Harvard University Press, 1983. Print.

Salam, Rula Kamal. Internal and External Wars: Mutilation as a Substitute for Expression in the Time of War as Studied in *The Story of Zahra* and *The Bullet Collection*. Beirut: American University of Beirut, 2004. Web. https://scholarworks.aub.edu.lb/handle/10938/6802 (Last accessed 12 Feb 2013)

Salem, Elise. *Constructing Lebanon: A Century of Literary Narratives*. Gainesville: University of Florida Press, 2003. Print.

Samman, Ghada. *Night of the First Billion*. Trans. Nancy N. Roberts. Syracuse, NY: Syracuse University Press, 2005. Print.

—. *Beirut Nightmares*. Trans. Nancy N. Roberts. London: Quartet Books, 1997. Print.

Sandoval, C. US Third World feminism: the Theory and Method of Oppositional Consciousness in the Postmodern World. *Genders* 10. Spring (1991): pp. 2–24. Print.

Schweickart, Patrocinio P. Reading ourselves: Toward a Feminist Theory of Reading. In *Feminisms: An Anthology of Literary Theory and Criticism*. Eds. Warhol, Robyn R. and Diane Price Herndl. New Brunswick, NJ: Rutgers University Press, 1997: pp. 609-634. Print.

Seife, Charles. *Zero: The Biography of a Dangerous Idea*. London: Souvenir Press Ltd, 2000. Print.

Shihada, Isham. Engendering War in Hanan Al Shaykh's The Story of Zahra. *Nebula*. 5.4 (2008): pp. 177-192. Print.

Shaw, Philip. *The Sublime*: *the New Critical Idiom*. Abingdon, UK: Routledge, 2006. Print.

Simon, Sherry *Gender in Translation: Cultural Identity and the Politics of Transmission*. London and New York: Routledge, Chapman and Hall, 1996. Print.

Sophocles. *Antigone*. Trans. Ian Johnston. British Columbia: Vancouver Island University, 2005. Web. https://records.viu.ca/~johnstoi/sophocles/antigone.htm (Last accessed 3 June 2012)

Starkey, Paul. *Modern Arabic Literature*. Edinburgh: Edinburgh University Press, 2006. Print.

Teloni, Maria-Chiara. Time and the Formation of the Human Person: A Comparison of Edith Stein's and Martin Heidegger's Thoughts. In *Timing and Temporality in Islamic Philosophy and Phenomenology of Life: Islamic Philosophy and Occidental Phenomenology in Dialogue*. Vol 3. Ed. Anna-Teresa Tymieniecka. Dordrecht, The Netherlands: Springer, 2007: pp. 225-266. Print.

Thompson, Stith. *Motif-Index of Folk-Literature: Index A-K : A Classification of Narrative Elements in Folktales, Ballads, Myths, Fables, Mediaeval Romances, Exempla, Fabliaux, Jest-Books, and Local Legends*. Bloomington: Indiana University Press, 2002. Print.

Traboulsi, Fawwaz. An Intelligent Man's Guide to Modern Arab Feminism. *Al-Raida*. XX; 100. 2003. 15-19. Web.

Tress, Daryl McGowan. The Metaphysical Science of Aristotle's *Generation of Animals* and its Feminist Critics. In *Feminism and Ancient Philosophy*. Ed. Julie K. Ward. New York: Routledge, 1996: pp. 31-50. Print.

Turner, Victor Witter. *Dramas, Fields, and Metaphors: Symbolic Action in Human Society*. New York City: Cornell University Press, 1975. Print.

Turshen, Meredeth. Women's War Stories. In *What Women Do in Wartime: Gender and Conflict in Africa*. Eds. Meredeth Turshen and Clotilde Twagiramariya. London: Zed Books, 1998: pp. 1-26. Print.

Tymieniecka, Anna-Teresa, Gholam Reza A'awani, and Nader El-Bizri, eds. *Timing and Temporality in Islamic Philosophy and Phenomenology of Life*. Dordrecht, The Netherlands: Springer, 2007. Print.

Valassopoulos, Anastasia. *Contemporary Arab Women Writers: Cultural Expression in Context*. New York: Routledge, 2007. Print.

Velde, H.T. Egyptian Hieroglyphs as Signs, Symbols and Gods. *Approaches to Inconography; Annual for Religious Iconography*. IV-V. Leiden: E.J. Brill, 1986. Print.

Venuti. Lawrence. The Translators Invisibility: A history of translation. London and New York: Routledge, 1995. Print.

Wahl, Jean A. *The Philosopher's Way*. New York: Oxford University Press, 1948. Memphis, TN: General Books LLC, reprinted 2012. Print.

Walker, Nancy A. *Feminist Alternatives: Irony and Fantasy in the Contemporary Novel by Women*. Jackson, MS: University Press of Mississippi, 1990. Print.

Walsh, Maria. Žižek, Deleuze, and the Feminine Cinematic Sublime. *Rhizomes*. 16. (2008): (n. pag.) Web. http://www.rhizomes.net/issue16/walsh/ (Last accessed 2 June 2013)

Wasilewska, Ewa. *Creation Stories of the Middle East*. London: Jessica Kingsley Publishers, 2000. Print.

Wasserstrom, Steven M. *Religion After Religion: Gershom Scholem, Mircea Eliade, and Henry Corbin at Eranos*. Princeton: Princeton University Press, 1999. Print.

Watts, Alan. *Myth and Ritual in Christianity*. New York: Evergreen, 1960. Print.

Wawrzinek, Jennifer. *Ambiguous Subjects: Dissolution and Metamorphosis in the Postmodern Sublime*. Amsterdam and New York: Rodopi, 2008. Print.

Wayne, T.K. *Feminist Writings from Ancient Times to the Modern World: A Global Sourcebook and History*. Santa Barbara, California: Greenwood, an imprint of ABC-CLIO. 2011. Print.

Weatherston, Rosemary. *When Sleeping Dictionaries Awaken: TheR e/turn of the Native Woman Informant.* Ann Arbor, MI: MPublishing, University of Michigan Library. 1997. Web. http://quod.lib.umich.edu/p/postid/ pid9999. 0001. 106? rgn=main;view=fulltext (Last accessed 3 June 2013)

Wiegman, Robyn. Academic Feminism against Itself. *NWSA Journal*. 14.2 (2002): pp. 18-37. The Johns Hopkins University Press. Web. http://www.jstor.org/stable/4316890 (Last accessed 3 June 2013)

Yaeger, Patricia. Toward a Female Sublime. In *Gender and Theory: Dialogues on Feminist Criticism*. Ed. Linda Kauffman. Oxford: Basil Blackwell, 1989: pp. 191-212. Print.

—. The 'Language of Blood': Toward a Maternal Sublime. *Genre* 25. (1995): pp. 5-24. Print.

Zeidan, Joseph. *Arab Women Novelists: The Formative Years and Beyond*. Albany: State University of New York Press, 1994. Print.

Zylinska, Joanna. Sublime Speculations: The Economy of the Gift in Feminist Ethics. *j spot. Journal of Social and Political Thought*. June 2001. Web. <http://www.yorku.ca/jspot/3/jzylinska.htm>. (Last accessed 9 Feb 2014)

السعداوي، نوال. *إمرأة عند نقطة الصفر*. الطبعة الثانية. القاهرة: مكتبة مدبولي، 2006

السمان،غادة. *ليلة المليار*. الطبعة الثالثة. بيروت: مطبعة دار الكتب، 2002

الشيخ،حنان. *حكاية زهرة*. الطبعة الرابعة. بيروت: دار الآداب ، 2004

العتابي،سعد. *الأدب الأنثوي بين القبول والرفض* 21 مايو 2011 ( 5 مايو 2013)
<http://www.aleflam.net/index.php?option=com_content&view=article&id=626:2011-05-21-12-35-05&catid=62:2010-01-18-14-55-43&Itemid=102>

مسعد،جوزيف. *كيف يجب ألا ندرس النوعَ الاجتماعيّ الجندر في العالم العربيّ* 07 أغسطس 2009 (25 أبريل 2013 )
<http://adabmag.com/node/223>

www.ingramcontent.com/pod-product-compliance
Lightning Source LLC
Chambersburg PA
CBHW080940040426
42444CB00015B/3380